FIT TO MA

An action plan for executives
performance in the face of today's increasingly hurried
and aggressive commercial lifestyle, and to remain healthy
and fit to manage

FIT TO MANAGE

An Executive's Guide to Peak Performance

Graham Jones

THORSONS PUBLISHING GROUP
Wellingborough, Northamptonshire

First Published 1988

British Library Cataloguing in Publication Data

Jones, Graham
Fit to manage : an executive's guide to
peak performance.
1. Executives. Health. Fit programmes
I. Title
RA776.5

ISBN 0-7225-1448-6

Published by Thorsons Publishers Limited,
Wellingborough, Northamptonshire,
NN8 2RQ, England

Printed in Great Britain by Biddles Limited, Guildford, Surrey

1 3 5 7 9 10 8 6 4 2

About the author

Graham Jones B.Sc. (Hons) is a freelance health and medical writer. His degree is in Human Biology, and he is a Member of the Royal Society of Health. He has written for a variety of publications, including *The Times, The Sunday Times, The Guardian, The Observer* and women's magazines such as *She* and *Over 21*. He contributes regularly to the medical press, and he writes the health column in the weekly general interest magazine *Celebrity*. He also writes the medical column in *Conference Britain*. Graham Jones is on the executive committee of the Medical Journalists Association, and is a member of the Medical Writers Group of the Society of Authors, and also of the American Medical Writers Association.

Contents

Acknowledgements

I would like to thank all the company doctors working in a wide range of industries, who gave me helpful information and answered my many questions. Thanks too are due to the staff of many hotels who provided data on special facilities, diets and so on. I would also like to thank: Alcohol Concern; AMI Hospitals; the British Heart Foundation; the British Safety Council; BUPA; Business Time System; Executive Health Screening; the Flora Project for Heart Disease Prevention; Health First; the National Westminster Bank; and the Scottish Health Education Group.

My thanks also go to my wife Cathy, who managed to suffer my devotion to the writing of this book without complaining.

Introduction

In recent years modern business life has become an even more hurried and aggressive affair. It is a fierce competitive world where positive results are wanted, and they are wanted now, if not sooner! Bosses are becoming more and more demanding, and, despite the protection of various statutes, the threat of instant dismissal and redundancy is always present. Life for today's executive is all 'cut and thrust'. Each day is busier than the last, and there never seems to be any light at the end of the tunnel.

We are constantly reminded about the need to succeed, and are lured into the trap of pushing harder and harder to be able to gain those things we have always wanted. Television only emphasizes the concept that being a success in business is equated with success in life. Indeed, in one 24-hour period towards the end of 1986, British television viewers could have watched no less than six hours of programmes whose content related to executives and their struggle for success. There was a one-hour soap opera in which a number of leading characters were either self-employed or were running small businesses and their business struggles formed much of the plot. Another programme looked at the difficulties of finding business premises, whilst a further programme investigated the impact of changes in the City of London. Yet another drama involved a highly successful, but brash, entrepreneur settling deals across the world and buying up companies worth millions of dollars. Then there was the drama series in which a married couple both ran separate businesses, where shares were being bought and sold, bank managers demanding loan repayments, and various deals were being struck—all in fifty minutes! On just one day, British television viewers could not have escaped thinking that executive life is meant to be fast, aggressive, competitive and, above all, successful.

Yet people who behave in this way—the hard, driving, competitive go-getters—are precisely the sort of people who are least likely to be able to benefit from their efforts. For people who adopt this behaviour pattern are those who tend to suffer more frequently from diseases of the heart and circulatory systems, and from stress, anxiety and so on. The ambitious, competitive executive is just the sort of person who will suffer a heart attack and die before being able to reap the rewards of a promising career.

Ill-health is not just a problem for individuals. It is a major difficulty for business and industry as well. Each day 1½ million workers out of the 21½ million people in full time employment in the UK will have a certificate from the doctor saying that they are unable to work. Each week 7 million working days are lost simply because of ill-health; that's a staggering total of almost 360 million working days lost each year due to sickness. These figures only take into account the 'certified days off'; in other words, they only apply to people who have a certificate · from their doctor. These figures do not take into account the people who may have had one or two days off for a cold, or to recover from a mighty hangover. No one can even begin to estimate what this might total. But what is known is that on average each worker has 17 days off work each year as a result of illness. The cost to industry is enormous. Many businesses are waking up to the idea that by promoting health and fitness amongst employees they might save money whilst increasing productivity and output.

Business executives are no different to the general population. They too have time off work as a result of illness, but many of the problems from which executives suffer can be avoided. Heart disease, for example, is a major cause of death. It is responsible for over one in every four deaths in the UK. Together with other circulatory disorders it accounts for around 60 million days off work each year. Medical research has shown that those people who behave like many modern executives, in a competitive go-getting way, stand a much higher than average chance of suffering from heart disease. Yet studies have also revealed that these people can modify their behaviour, reduce their risk of heart disease, and still be a success in their careers or their business.

Another major reason for time off work is disorders of the muscular system, or problems with bones and joints. These tend to occur in those people who sit down for much of the day, like office workers. The disorders account for almost 58 million days off work each year. Here, again, many of these difficulties are preventable. Good chairs, desks at the correct height, good lighting and so on, have all been shown to play a part in cutting down the amount of musculo-skeletal problems amongst people at work.

A further 50 million days each year are taken off work because of 'mental disorders'. This covers a wide range of problems, but it has been estimated that at least 40 million days are related to stress, a seemingly growing problem amongst today's modern executives. More appears to have been written about 'executive stress' in recent years than on many other aspects of health at work. Whilst there is no denying it is a problem, it is not the only condition which affects the modern manager. Three executives out of every four, like the general population, will die of either cardiovascular disease or cancer.

In many instances these diseases bring early death, without people reaching their true life expectancy. Today British men can expect to live until they are 70, whilst women have a life expectancy of 77 years. However, many people do not live this long, and sadly, many of the conditions from which they died could have been prevented.

This book is a guide to help in the prevention of disease. It will not stop anyone from getting heart disease, or contracting cancer, for example, but it should help to reduce the risks. Executives tend to be healthier than the average person. They consult their doctor less frequently than is the average. But the executive is now living in the increasingly difficult world of business where the modern pressures of commerce and industry combine to force managers into patterns of behaviour which are not good for their health.

Executives exhibit tendencies which make them more likely to suffer heart disease; they live under constant pressure often making it impossible to find time for a balanced meal; they travel frequently and have to sleep in hotel beds which do not support their backs; they have to face the strains of being away from their homes and their families for days on end; they spend long hours in meetings and cannot find time to exercise; and they may often drink too much alcohol. Altogether, modern business life is taking its toll on the health of today's executive.

This book is therefore not only a guide as to how medical conditions may be prevented, it is also a manual for the modern executive who wants to obtain and maintain health. It provides an overall plan which will allow busy executives to continue with their successful careers, whilst reducing their risks of disease and avoiding medical complaints.

But do not fool yourself into believing that by simply following the advice and suggestions in this book that you will be certain to be less likely to develop particular conditions. No book can make that promise. Whilst the health plans outlined in this book should help cut down your chances of the most common problems, none of the advice should be put into operation without the approval of your doctor. There may be a particular reason why you should not take some of the advice, but more likely is the fact that your doctor will help you tailor the health plans to help you specifically.

Hopefully, by using the health plans in this book, together with discussions with medical advisors, executives will be able to lead a healthier and happier life, whilst still being able to aim for the top in business.

1
A Healthy Mind

Unless you are extremely lucky it is not possible to achieve lasting good health without putting your mind to it. Our bodies are constructed from a unique set of instructions embedded in 46 chromosomes—23 passed on from each of our parents. The chromosomes contain a large number of different 'genes'. Genes are nothing more than groups of chemicals arranged in such a way as to 'instruct' our cells to do certain things, such as make a particular protein. These genes are scattered all over our chromosomes, and there are hundreds of thousands of them. Many of these genes, though, are unique. Although we all carry similar genetic instructions which tell our bodies such things as where our feet go, and what muscles should be made out of, there are many genes which can differ between individuals—the colour of our eyes is but one example. It is because of this possibility of variation that we all suffer from different diseases. If we were all identical in our make-up, and lived in similar conditions then we would, in all probability, die from the same cause. However we are different, and consequently we vary in the sort of diseases and medical conditions from which we suffer.

Scientists are only just beginning to unravel the genetic mysteries which explain why certain individuals suffer from particular diseases, but there are already clues which indicate that some types of people have a genetic make-up which makes them more prone to specific conditions. For example, people who have Down's Syndrome—an error in genetic make-up—are now known to be more likely to suffer from certain infections than individuals who do not have this disorder. This shows that changes in our genes can be responsible for alterations in our susceptibility to disease.

It seems logical to assume that genetic alterations which are less dramatic and serious than those which lead to Down's Syndrome, may also influence our likelihood of suffering from particular conditions. This would imply that some people will be born with genetic instructions which give them a much higher risk of suffering from heart disease, whilst others will be more likely to die of cancer, for example. However, most of us will never be able to know precisely what our genetic instructions are, so we must adopt as healthy a lifestyle as possible to avoid as many of the potential problems as we can. To do this we need to take positive action to change the bad habits we may have developed over the years, not an easy task and one which requires changing our attitude of mind if we are to achieve the necessary motivation. No plan for healthy living stands any chance of being helpful unless we are prepared to put our minds to it. The genetic instructions contained in our cells will not be overridden by mere hope. We have to make a determined effort.

Millions of people know that they should not smoke, yet they do, and no amount of talk about will-power will help them stop. It would probably help if doctors were able to pick out those people at higher risk of certain diseases because of their genetic make-up, but this is a long way off in the future. Until then we must all assume that each of us is at risk of the most common disorders. There are still people, though, who smoke cigarettes and claim, for example, that their Great Uncle Fred used to smoke 60 a day, never had a day off work, and died peacefully in his sleep at the ripe old age of 98. There may be a few people like this around, whose genetic make-up has enabled their bodies, somehow, to have a lower risk of developing the diseases associated with cigarette smoking. However, the fact that they were able to smoke heavily without any apparent ill-effect is not proof that smoking is harmless as far as the rest of us are concerned.

The same is true for people who claim that unlimited amounts of alcohol do not lead to any problems because their Aunty Maud had a bottle of gin every day, and two on Sundays. There are such people, perhaps, but they are rare, and they are genetically different. People who use these sort of examples are merely giving excuses to back up their own ill-advised behaviour patterns. These people cannot or will not give the amount of psychological effort that is required to improve their own health. They do not have the will-power.

A blanket statement such as 'smoking is bad for you' is less likely to produce a response than specifically showing a group of executives that medical evidence suggests they stand a much higher risk of smoking-related diseases than skilled manual workers because the effects of the smoke can combine with known hormonal effects in executives to produce heart disease. Telling executives that they stand a much higher chance of heart disease as a result of smoking in this way is more likely to get this group of people to stop smoking, because their will-power will have been mobilized.

Inspiring the motivation to change is one of the hardest things to do. Why should a 30-year-old sales administrator change his happy way of life; after all, he may say, it is doing no harm at the moment. Or a 40-year-old lady bank manager might think she does not need to change her hectic lifestyle just yet, because she appears to be in perfect health.

Sadly, these people are wrong. All the bad habits which affect our health do so collectively, and additively, over a long timespan. We do not suddenly become at risk of a heart attack at the age of 55, that risk has been building up over the years. We do not suddenly get cirrhosis of the liver, it is something which occurs as a result of many years of heavy drinking. Young executives who drink heavily claiming they will cut down as they get older have already started to damage their livers. Healthy living should begin at any age, in fact the earlier the better.

However, trying to convince young executives that they should change their lifestyles in order to improve their

health and reduce their risks of diseases is not a simple
matter. The degree of success depends upon the
willingness of these people to co-operate. They need a
healthy mental status to overcome the excuses they have
used for so long to put off taking any positive action to
improve their overall health. Obtaining such a healthy
status requires clear, positive thought, a willingness to
believe in yourself, and a relaxed, unstressed attitude.
Sadly, it is the stress in an executive's life which often
prevents the existence of a healthy mind necessary to
embark on a plan for healthy living.

One way of motivating people into action is the use of
shocking statistics. Something like 70,000 executives
under the age of 64 die each year. Managers, for example,
have a 20 per cent greater chance of dying of cancer of the
colon than the general population. Doctors are 15 per cent
more likely to die of cirrhosis of the liver than the general
population. Four men in every 1,000 under the age of 55
die of heart disease. Almost 160,000 people die of heart
disease each year, and some 30,000 of these are men in
executive-type occupations under the age of 64. That
means that almost one in five of all heart disease deaths
are in male executives before retirement. Should you need
any more motivation to think about changing your
lifestyle in order to improve your health, then the
statistical tables of 'Occupational Mortality' published by
the UK's Office of Population Censuses and Surveys
provides some chilling reading.

Perhaps these sorts of figures are not enough to
motivate you into trying to improve your mind, and so
your overall health status. One reason you may give for
not being able to set your mind to the task is sheer lack of
time. A common claim from executives is that they simply
do not have the time to follow any rigid health-promoting
programmes. They know that they ought to do it, but
there just isn't the time available. There are only 24 hours
in each and every day, after all!

Time management

Managing time to the best effect is an important aspect of executive life, and is sadly one area of professional work which is often neglected. Time management has a number of positive advantages. Firstly it increases the efficiency of an executive—work gets performed more effectively and deadlines are reached. Secondly time management avoids time-wasting and so allows executives those extra minutes each day to perform those essential health-promoting tasks such as exercise or relaxation. Time management also has a very positive health effect in its own right. It can be extremely helpful in avoiding pressure, strain, and can thus reduce the oft-mentioned syndrome of 'executive stress'. As has already been mentioned, removing stress is an important aspect of obtaining the positive and healthy frame of mind which is a prerequisite to improving overall health.

Stress in work situations comes from a number of different sources, of which poor time management is thought to be highly significant. However, the phenomenon of 'executive stress' is in itself somewhat misleading. Executives do not suffer from any special form of stress, and stress is not due to overwork, or responsible work. Stress can equally occur in young mothers at home looking after children, in the teenage unemployed, or in a production line worker at a car factory. Stress is not an executive disease. However, the working environment of executives, and their behaviour patterns can lead to stress. So what is stress and how can time management help alleviate it?

Stress

All of us, at some time or another, believe that we are 'under stress'. Delving further into this simple phrase we reveal a whole host of problems. Firstly what exactly is stress, how is it defined?

Stress was first introduced into the medical world in

1926 by a Prague medical student, Hans Selye. He claimed that certain people suffered various physical symptoms which tended to occur together. He used the word 'stress' to describe basic wear and tear which led to this group of symptoms.

However, it was not until the mid-1970s, when Selye was a professor in Montreal, Canada, that his concepts of stress and disease became more established in the medical community, largely as a result of books written by Selye based on his thoughts and findings over the years. Professor Selye defined stress as being the response to various outside demands made upon the body. In other words, something which makes us frightened, for example, is a 'stressor', and the biological reaction which our body produces in response to this stressor is the stress, which in turn leads to the feelings of fear.

Although many psychologists have attempted to expand this definition of stress over the years, their attempts have proved futile. Stress is not an entity which can be generalized. What causes a stress response in one executive may not even affect another. Some people will feel under pressure with only half the amount of work to do than the person in the next office. Stress, its causes, and responses to it, are entirely individual. What can be said in general terms, though, is that the symptoms of stress tend to be similar, and these are the symptoms which Selye described as long ago as 1926.

However, these symptoms are only produced when there is an *excess* of stress. Low levels of stress can be positively beneficial, stimulating people into action and helping executives work at peak performance. But if the stress levels go too high, then symptoms set in and people can be said to be 'suffering from stress'. If you happen to be an executive, then such symptoms are labelled 'executive stress', although this is nothing more than a fashionable term. Where for example are all the individuals suffering from 'dole queue stress' or 'farm labourer stress'? Indeed, during the research for this book one company doctor revealed than many of the managers working is his company felt that they ought to be suffering from 'executive stress' simply because they had heard so much about it!

However, other doctors confirmed that many executives do show symptoms of too much stress. These include headaches, nausea, low appetite, indigestion, tiredness, irritability, low sex drive, dizziness, and generalized feelings of failure. (A fuller list of common symptoms of stress is shown in Table 1 on pages 21 and 22.)

There is a sound scientific basis for the production of these symptoms and some understanding of this can help executives understand how stress is linked to other disorders, such as heart disease.

The biology of stress

The stress response is triggered off by an outside stimulus. It may be something physical which stresses us, such as someone standing on our foot, or it may be an emotional stimulus such as a boss in a temper, or an imaginary fear. In any event the brain is geared into action. In a complicated manner involving various parts of the brain we subconsciously 'decide' whether or not the stimulus is in any way threatening. If it is perceived as a threat then the stress response proper begins.

Table 1
COMMON SYMPTOMS OF STRESS

- Irritability
- Tiredness
- Indecisiveness
- Anger
- Low sex drive
- Poor appetite
- Indigestion
- Nausea

- Constipation
- Diarrhoea
- Dizziness
- Headaches
- Neck pain
- Insomnia
- Breathlessness
- Chest pain
- Sweating
- Lack of concentration
- Lack of sense of humour

A number of chemicals are released within the nervous system to prepare the body to cope with the perceived threat. The most important of these are adrenalin, and nor-adrenalin—sometimes known as epinephrine and nor-epinephrine, particularly by American scientists. These hormones co-ordinate certain changes in the body enabling us either to fight off the threat or to run away from it; this is known as the 'fight or flight response'. Blood is diverted from the gut to the muscles where it can be of more use, and digestion is halted a a result. Breathing becomes more rapid ready to provide a boost of oxygen should it be needed. The blood pressure rises, and the number of chemicals and cells which help blood clotting are increased in case they too are required. The kidneys almost stop processing urine, and there is an urgent need to empty the bladder so that we can run or fight without any problem. Glucose and fats are released from our stores so that plentiful energy supplies are available. Concentration becomes acute, with all extraneous thoughts pushed aside. Blood is diverted away from our sexual organs and thoughts of sexual activity are restricted. Within seconds of the pumping out of adrenalin the body is ready to take on anything.

If the threat is real, such as a manic hippopotamus roaring down the High Street, then our bodies are perfectly prepared to deal with the situation. We run away with relative ease because energy has been provided, our muscles, heart, and lungs have been prepared for the effort, and our brain has been concentrated on the situation by kicking out needless thoughts. Once we have run away from the hippo and the danger is over, nor-adrenalin is released and the effects of adrenalin are removed, our muscles return to normal, our blood pressure drops, and so on.

But what if the threat is not a real one? What if we have imagined that the boss will be angry if we do not do a particular item of work on time? The adrenalin will still rise, and so too will blood pressure, the levels of fats in our bloodstream, breathing rate, and so on. Because the threat is imaginary and has no obvious end, the body is unable to remove its 'fight or flight' response so quickly. It is this simple fact which can lead to stress symptoms. The lack of a real end to a perceived threat can allow the stress response to continue for long periods. Result—we become overstressed.

So perceived threats can lead to increases in blood pressure, higher levels of blood fats and sugars, changes in digestion, alterations in blood supply to the brain, increases of blood supply to the muscles, and increased breathing rates. In the long run, the continuation of these different states can lead to symptoms. The excess blood supply in the brain may be at the root of headaches, the muscles all tensed and ready for action will lead to muscular aches and pains, and the halting of digestion may cause upsets like indigestion. Thus there is sound biological evidence to show that stress in our lives can lay behind physical complaints. Stress is not 'all in the mind', as some people, particularly hard pushy bosses, would have us believe. But, our minds can have an important influence over the likelihood of stress leading to symptoms.

The imaginary stresses of our daily lives tend to be

generated in our emotions as a result of us not thinking out clearly the possibilities. We become stressed because we think that the boss will be angry if we do not complete a report on time, and we push ourselves harder to complete the task, which only compounds the stresses. Rarely, do we sit down and ask ourselves, 'Will the boss really be angry? If I tell him I need more time to do the report as it is more important to do last month's sales figures first, then he may well commend me for my logical thought.' Usually, though, we soldier on, increasing the pressure on our work life as a result of our own actions and imaginings. This is where time management can play a significant role in reducing job-related stress.

Careful planning of our daily lives can significantly reduce our stress. If each day is planned on a flexible basis we know exactly what has to be done, when it has to be done, how much time is available to perform the task, who will help perform it, and so on.

Many executives have a carefully organized diary with dates and times of meetings listed. Whilst this makes them look, and feel, efficient, it is only a half-hearted attempt at managing their day-to-day activities. All of those meetings will need preparation, trips away from the office will need planning, and work itself will need slotting in between the appointments. To make life more efficient, it is vital that executives timetable everything.

Educational establishments are run according to well-defined and carefully planned timetables. Students could be told 'here is a list of what you need to know for all of your exams, so take the next two years to learn it.' However, the likelihood of any student being able to learn the required amount is low. There are too many other distractions. Educational timetables ensure that students follow a programmed course of learning so that they have been able to study all of the items necessary prior to examination. Executive life should really be no different.

Managers, administrators, salesmen, and so on would all benefit from producing a timetable which allows them to fit in all of the work they need to do each week, but which is also flexible enough to take into account unforeseen circumstances. However, there is a significant reason why schools have timetables and many executives do not.

Schools have predefined targets to achieve, they have specific goals—usually examinations. The trouble with many executives, according to some business commentators, is the simple fact that they do not set themselves goals or targets. Companies will have general targets— they may want to double turnover, or reduce staff expenses by 10 per cent, or to begin exporting within 6 months—but rarely do individuals set themselves their own goals to achieve within the company's own strategy.

Stress is frequently caused by people not knowing 'where they are going'. It is created by a large degree of personal uncertainty. Consequently demands upon an executive's time begin to conflict and stress increases until symptoms appear. If executives can set their own goals and then plan their time to achieve these aims, the conflicts are less likely to arise and so is excess stress.

For example, an executive might decide that by the end of a given week a report needs writing, a mail shot needs organizing, and an analysis of sales figures needs careful reading. Without a flexible timetable to achieve these aims these projects will get mixed in with any other work which happens to turn up on the executive's desk. By the middle of the week increasing demands will be made upon the poor executive and it is quite probable that by the end of the week stress has set in because the manager has not achieved what ought to have been done.

With a flexible timetable, though, such increasing pressure and mounting conflicts can be reduced. The executive can plan to devote the first day to dealing with the weekend's post and initiating the planning of the mail shot by delegating a more junior member of staff to perform the preliminary stages of the work.

The second day can be devoted to discussing the mail shot project and doing research for the report writing. The third day might be left partly free to allow for further work on the mail shot if necessary, or to gain more information for the report. The remainder of this day might have been previously committed to a departmental meeting. The hour before this meeting can be timetabled to read the briefing notes, and do some background research for one of the items on the agenda. The remainder of the week can be devoted to writing the report and finalizing the mail shot, together with time available to deal with any unforeseen items that have turned up.

If the manager has allowed, say, an hour each morning to deal with the post, and an hour each afternoon to deal with staff problems, the week will have been planned, and flexible enough to allow all of the work to be completed. Many executives might think that they do this sort of planning, but it really needs to be written down so that it can be analysed and adapted to the changing needs of the work. The timetable should also take into account personal and home life; it would be a poor timetable that programmed a meeting which could be extended by an hour or so on the same day as an important social dinner engagement twenty miles from home. In addition a weekly timetable which doesn't take into account monthly meetings, or quarterly reviews, annual reports and so on will also be inadequate. An executive's timetable needs to be a well organized and carefully planned programme which covers all aspects of day to day life—and it should allow time each day and each week to assess the timetable and make changes as appropriate.

A number of specially prepared diary systems are available which allow executives to plan and have all the information at their fingertips which helps in this planning, such as telephone numbers, information on key accounts, expenses forms, management forms, data on world holidays, and much more. These are considerably more expensive than the average appointment diary, but they are becoming increasingly popular with companies.

A carefully planned day, week, or month, can allow executives to reduce the pressure on their time. Increasing demand on time creates pressure because an executive begins to feel overburdened with work. 'Everything gets on top of me' is the usual response to the situation and less work is performed because of the increasingly

A HEALTHY MIND

frustrating situation. The time pressures then become acute since the reduced amount of work caused by frustration over lack of time only further reduces the time available. A vicious circle is established and executives do not achieve all they would hope for. A timetable reduces the pressures since time is allotted specifically to each task.

According to James Noon, a consultant in business and management and development, and an author of books on time management, a manager generally spends only 30 per cent of the available working time on matters of importance. Professor Cary Cooper, one of Britain's leading authorities on stress, has claimed in a number of books that conflicting demands on time are a major cause of stress amongst executives. It therefore seems logical to suggest that by using their time better, managers would be able to become more efficient as well as less stressed.

However, pressures on time are not the only source of stress upon today's executive. Domestic problems can also lead to stress symptoms.

Home life

Psychological research and various surveys have demonstrated that we cannot separate our working lives from our home lives. The two are intertwined, and quite ordinary work pressures can appear very stressful if our home lives are in any way upset. Indeed, one company doctor who provided information for this book said that many cases of so-called 'executive stress' actually originate with problems in home life.

Executives may live in a variety of home situations. They may be single, living alone, or single but sharing a house, or living with parents. People in executive positions may be married, they may have children who are young, or grown up. Executives can be male, female, and they may be heterosexual, homosexual, or bisexual. Altogether, it is almost impossible to generalize about today's executive. About ten years ago it would have been acceptable to say that an executive was most likely to be a married man with two children. Today that is not true. It is therefore no longer possible to say that the domestic problems of executives tend to revolve around a wife and children.

Home-based problems which can lead to symptoms of stress can be as varied as executives themselves. Unlike the office environment, where time pressures are a prime candidate for causing stress amongst large cross-sections of managers and administrators, there can be no such generalization for stress-inducing home situations. One executive may suffer from stress as a result of the difficulties of coping with combining a responsible high-powered job with the needs of growing children. Another worker may be finding it stressful living as a homosexual in a society which largely condemns such people.

No executive who suffers from stress does so simply as a result of pressure at work. Whilst work itself is a major contributory factor, the home life of any worker can also be a prime cause of stress and can lead to stress-related symptoms. There is, though, one fairly common cause of home stress which is due to the job itself. And this relates, again, to time management.

Executives frequently take work home. The office may not be free of interruptions, the telephone may be constantly ringing for example, and a quiet evening at home can provide time to concentrate. However, taking work home does not allow the executive to 'switch-off'; work is ever present. In addition, taking work home reduces the amount of time available for being with the family, or a husband, or wife, or boyfriend or girlfriend. These people can become upset, rightly, at the reduced time available for spending together and can become angry and critical. The result is that the executive feels under increased pressure. For not only are the various aspects of working life all making demands on his available time, but now home life is also making increased demands on that time. The demands from home for increased attention conflict with the demands from work for extra effort. In the end, the executive feels overburdened, and stress sets in.

Taking work home can also lead to stress in other ways. Whilst hours spent working may lead partners to demand more time from a busy executive, it may also lead to arguments, probably over quite trivial things. The executive's partner may not necessarily make demands over time, but may still feel threatened as a result of the extra work. A relationship may change because a partner feels that the executive is 'married to the job', and that they have become secondary to the work. This can lead to a breakdown in the relationship between two people. Indeed, it is no surprise to learn that executives suffering from stress repeatedly report that their sex lives are not what they used to be.

Taking work home can also lead to arguments over money. The executive whose partner buys something, no matter how necessary, may be chastised by a harassed manager claiming, 'I have to do all these extra hours working just to buy things like that?' Arguments quickly follow about the family's cash flow situation!

Then there are arguments created by imaginary thoughts from an executive's partner. A man, whose wife is a success in business and is being rapidly promoted, may believe that he is less adequate than her. Alternatively, a wife, whose husband has an attractive young secretary may feel that she is under threat from the other woman. In either instance, the threat is not real, but the belief can create a strain in the relationship, lead to arguments, and cause stress symptoms in the executive.

Stress at home can also be created by simple money worries, like, can the telephone bill be paid? Or stress may be due to concerns over sick relatives, or the education of children. Without doubt, the pressure of home life makes an enormous impact upon today's executive, and no manager, administrator, salesman, or whatever, should ignore the possibility that domestic problems are contributing to stress symptoms.

The work-home 'interface' is an important one. As we have seen, work can create problems at home, and domestic difficulties can lead to problems at work. An executive whose mind is still running over last night's row, will not be able to settle to his work properly. Neither will an executive who is permanently worried about how to pay the gas bill.

However, many stresses from home are created by the rigours of executive life, taking work home being one of the main areas for concern. Business trips can also take their toll, leading to concerns over time being spent with children, or to relationship difficulties as a result of jealousy from partners.

If home-created stress is produced as a result of working patterns like these then time management can certainly help. An executive who efficiently apportions time may never need to take work home, and so may avoid many of the stresses which that would cause. However, even with efficient time management it may be necessary for some executives to take papers home to the dining-room table. The office may be too noisy to allow concentration, for example, or a meeting has been sprung upon you and some background reading is necessary. Whatever the reason, time management can still help, especially by reducing conflicting demands from partners and the family. An executive who clearly states that, for example, office work will be done at home every Thursday evening, will be able to have an uninterrupted evening, with no pressure from partners or other family members, since they will be aware that other evenings are available for time together.

Time management will allow executives to spend more time with friends, partners, and families. In addition to reducing the stress produced by conflicting demands from work and home, the chance to spend more hours each week in the company of friends and family is helpful in reducing stress in itself. It allows executives more time to take their mind off work. So, even with the pressures of home life, time management is an important aspect of reducing stress.

Time management takes on a new meaning, though, for many women managers. In addition to the conflicting demands of home and work, which are increased if the female executive's partner does not do his share of the domestic chores, there is the additional problem of deciding if and when to start a family. Professor Cary Cooper at the University of Manchester Institute of Science and Technology has found in his research that this dilemma is one of the highest causes of stress in women executives. Often, women are put in the position of having to decide whether to give up a promising career to start a family, or suffer the criticism of partners and relatives for their decision not to have children. The pressures from other family members, especially mothers, should not be underestimated, say psychologists. These can create severe levels of stress in women executives.

One way out of the problem is for businesses in general to be more accommodating to the women who do decide to start a family. A pioneer in this area has been the National Westminster Bank which has a special scheme for women who are of management potential. This offers women who join the scheme the chance to take up to five years off work to start their families and then rejoin the company to carry on in their careers. All that the bank asks, is that these women work for a minimum of two weeks every year during their break from full-time employment. The women on this scheme are kept in touch with what is going on in the company and the banking world by regular newsletters and meetings.

Sadly, though, this sort of example is rare, and many women have to face the difficult choice of family or career. Discussing the situation with partners will help, and women should never be afraid of approaching bosses to see if a scheme like the one NatWest operates could be worked out for them. Without some means of defusing the pressures on women they may well suffer from the stress-related symptoms such as headaches, tiredness, and so on, which are common to all people who are suffering from stress. However, women also suffer from other stress-related symptoms which are not experienced by their male colleagues.

Stress is a common cause of the absence of menstrual

periods. This is not quite so surprising as it may sound. The hormonal changes of the 'fight or flight' response will inhibit menstruation in order to help the woman deal with the perceived threat effectively. However, the absence of periods, or amenorrhoea as doctors call it, can in itself be extremely distressing. Women wonder if they are pregnant, and if not they may imagine all sorts of possible causes including such serious matters as cancer. This only adds to the stress. A pregnancy testing kit in the bathroom may be helpful in putting a woman's mind at rest if she is worried, and a trip to the GP should be arranged if the problem continues for more than a couple of months so that other causes of amenorrhoea, such as hormone irregularities, can be eliminated. But women should also be made aware that amenorrhoea is strongly linked to stress, and can also be linked to exercise.

Another problem which women can suffer as a result of stress is painful intercourse. Sexual difficulties are also a source of problems for male executives under stress.

Sex

Sexual relationships can be the source of considerable levels of stress. An executive who feels under strain, and is bringing work home, is unlikely to be very interested in sex. Indeed, psychologists who study stress say that a reduced interest in sex is one of the first signs that a person is beginning to suffer from stress.

The trouble is that this lack of sexual arousal can also increase the stress, since the partner feels neglected and may even as a result begin to ask for more sexual activity, thus providing a conflicting demand on the time and attention of the executive. Busy executives do not, in general, avoid sex deliberately, or due to some deep-seated psychological reason. Usually, the avoidance of sex is simply due to the fact that the executive is tired, or feels that not enough time is available. Pressure from partners to engage in sexual activity can only increase the problem. Some executives may 'go through the motions' of sex without really enjoying it, whilst others will just say no.

Sex therapists agree that the best way to take the pressure off the situation is to stop trying to have sex altogether. Both partners should realize that their sex life is not what it used to be, and should talk about the difficulty. Then they should agree that sexual intercourse is 'off limits'. This removes any pressure on the executive, who can then take time to re-explore his, or her, sexual identity. The first step is to go back to loving each other. Showing each other affection, buying small presents, and simply being interested in each other can open up the relationship that was beginning to suffer from difficulties. Sex therapists then advise that sexual partners should simply learn to touch each other, to explore each other's body through massage.

Going away for a so-called 'dirty weekend' with your sexual partner is one way of breaking the run of the mill routine of lovemaking, which can often lie behind an executive's 'boredom' with sex. However, once again, the effective use of work time will be the only way in which executives will be able to find the hours needed to explore a new and exciting sex life.

Finding time for a good sex life is beneficial in itself. Sex is a great relaxer, and is an excellent means of alleviating stress, and the worries of the day. A good sex life is often a boon to executives who feel under pressure, but sadly, because of the stresses of the modern working world, too few executives apparently enjoy a fruitful sexual relationship.

Sex, though, should not be ignored by any executive who wishes to reduce the stresses of life. Not only is it an enjoyable pastime, but there is also sound biological evidence to link the physical activity of sex with a reduction in stress. Like any muscular exercise, sexual activity causes small amounts of hormones called endorphins to be released. These are morphine-like chemicals which produce the same sort of emotional lift as might be obtained from a couple of alcoholic drinks. This 'high' leads to a generalized feeling of well-being and also reduces depression. This is why sex, and other forms of muscular exercise, can be so helpful in reducing stress.

Exercise

Many fitness fanatics seem to go on and on about the
benefits of exercise. One week, exercise is claimed as a
cure-all, and another it is only good for slimming down
the waistline. A week later, no doubt, someone will
debunk the entire theory and claim that exercise is
dangerous. Indeed, the fashion for jogging, which may
reduce the risk of heart disease, has come in for criticism
because of middle-aged men who have died suddenly
whilst out jogging. What some of the people who criticize
the benefits of jogging seem to fail to tell us is the fact that
many of the 'jogging deaths' may be accidents—the
runners could have been knocked down by careless
drivers.

In reality, as we shall see in following chapters, carefully
programmed exercise has been proven time and time
again to be extremely beneficial, despite what the critics
might say. And the benefits of exercise have probably not
been emphasized sufficiently well in the reduction of
stress.

Exercise causes the release of the morphine-like
hormones, endorphins, which produce the emotional
high which many runners report. These lead to a feeling of
relaxation. Exercise does not have to be vigorous or
prolonged to produce the beneficial effects of endorphins.
One hour's worth of exercise spread through the week is
about the right level for most of us, say many health and
medical experts. Three periods of about 20 minutes each
week is all that is needed to achieve the multitudinous
benefits of exercise.

How can a busy executive find that vital hour each week
to exercise in a bid to help control stress? Here again,
time management will be of major help, but even with
effective time planning, there still may not be enough
hours in each day to fit everything in. If this is the case,
then executives need to resort to alternative methods of

exercising. Firstly, use your legs!

It may sound silly, but executives tend not to use their legs anywhere near enough. They go by car, or by taxi, they use lifts and escalators, and some of them even have chauffeurs so they don't have to trouble their feet muscles to operate the car's pedals! By using your legs you can begin to achieve some of the benefits of exercise. Use stairs rather than lifts or escalators, walk to nearby meetings rather than use taxis, and walk around the office to talk to the staff about work, rather than use the internal telephone system. These sorts of activities will all help by exercising some muscles.

A number of firms now have their own gymnasiums, or ready access to one. According to *The Economist* magazine, some 20,000 companies in the United States have set up their own health and fitness clubs, and in the UK a number of leading firms are installing their own facilities as well. The Abbey National Building Society, for example, has two fitness centres, and a company called 'Fitness for Industry' will install gyms for interested organizations.

Try to arrive at work half an hour early a couple of days a week so you can use the gym's facilities before starting a day's work. You will probably find this easier than using the gym at the end of the day when the attractions of going home are much more persuasive. A work-out in the gym may well put you in a good frame of mind to face the day as a result of the relaxing effects of the increased endorphins in your system. A half-hour in the gym may be a good prescription for starting a day when difficult meetings are due to take place, or a major project needs tackling.

There are a number of other factors which can lead to stress which should be dealt with simultaneously if any real attempt at reducing such stress is to be successful.

Diet

The old saying that 'we are what we eat' was never meant

to be taken literally. But it is undoubtedly true that all foods have a profound effect on our bodies and our health. Each foodstuff is composed of a unique set of chemicals, all of which have differing effects on our bodies. The caffeine in certain drinks, for example, increases the activity of our kidneys and therefore makes us urinate more frequently. The vitamin B contained in red meat and fresh vegetables, as another example, is used in the manufacture of our red blood cells. And the calcium contained in milk is utilized every day to replace that which is lost from our bones. Food is not just for the provision of energy, it has a complex role to play in all of the body's systems. It is therefore of no surprise to learn that foodstuffs can also have an effect on the brain.

Certain food additives, for example, can change behaviour patterns. The bestselling book *E for Additives* by Maurice Hanssen reveals a number of chemicals added to foods which can cause changes in behaviour—the most widely reported of which is an orange dye called tartrazine which is thought to lie behind some cases of hyperactivity in children. More commonly, coffee is widely renowned to be a stimulant, keeping people awake at night, for example. There is no doubt that foods can and do affect all of our bodies, including our brains.

It therefore seems logical to assume that what doctors describe as a healthy balanced diet, one which is known to have beneficial effects in the prevention of heart disease, gastrointestinal disease, and also possibly of certain cancers, may well also be kind to our brains. A diet such as that prescribed to prevent heart disease may well have the right kind of nutrients in it to help reduce the effects of the stresses in our lives. This is a difficult theory to prove, and one that has not yet been adequately studied.

However, research on 800,000 schoolchildren in the United States has shown that academic performance is improved and bad behaviour is less when a healthy diet is adopted, compared to when 'convenience' foods are eaten. This implies that there is a link between what we eat and how we perform psychologically. As we shall see in later chapters, eating sensibly considerably reduces the risks of heart disease, disorders of the stomach and intestines, and certain cancers. So eating a healthy diet in a bid to reduce the effects of stress will have beneficial spin-off effects in terms of the general health of both body and mind.

Eating sensibly as an executive is easier said than done! Meals frequently have to be eaten on trains, or in flight, and restaurants and hotels tempt the executive with sumptuous delights and all sorts of fat-laden sauces on their menus. Choosing the right hotel or restaurant is a start. Most hotels will cater for people requesting special menus, such as diabetics, or vegetarians, and now there are increasing numbers of hotels which are including 'healthy' foods on their menus. For example, Crest Hotels, De Vere Hotels, Embassy Hotels, Holiday Inns, Ladbroke Hotels, and Sheraton Hotels, all offer menus which contain healthy meals. (This does not imply that the rest of the menu is completely unhealthy, just that some of the items in the general menu, such as rich sauces, may not be too good for people who have to be particularly conscious about their health.) Large business hotels, such as the Grosvenor House and the Inter-Continental in London's Park Lane, both have special 'healthy breakfast' menus which are certainly more appropriate than the eggs, bacon, sausages, and so on which is traditional in many hotels.

Restaurants are also coming round to providing healthy, balanced meals, and it is possible to spot a good wholesome meal on even some of the most sauce-laden menus around. For example, when looking at a restaurant menu, look for foods which you know to be healthy— chicken, fish, liver and so on—and avoid those with rich sauces that may contain lashings of cream and booze! Choose a side-salad, instead of chipped potatoes, and ask for a wholemeal roll, rather than white bread. Simple things like these can allow a healthy meal to be chosen, without causing any fuss or embarrassment. It seems that the executive's favourite lunchtime dish is still steak and chips, but the calories and cholesterol contained in such a meal will not do an executive much good if it is eaten on a regular basis. Choosing other foods is not at all difficult, it just requires the right attitude of mind, a bit of will-power, as mentioned earlier on in this chapter. In addition, light, easily digested lunches, will be more likely to reduce the risks of stress during the afternoon than a heavy meal which might make an executive suffer from indigestion and tiredness.

A sensible approach to diet will help reduce executive stress, and as explained in the next chapters will be of major help in other areas. However, simple adherence to healthy eating will not be sufficient to deal with stress on its own.

Relaxation

No matter how many steps an executive takes to avoid stress there is always the risk that stress-related symptoms may develop. This is because, as explained earlier, we are all genetically different, our susceptibility to particular problems is individual and there is the possibility that for some of us the problem of stress may even break through the preventative barriers we set up against it. Indeed, even if an executive follows this chapter's plan of time management, a fruitful home life, a good sexual relationship, exercising and healthy eating, the problems he has encountered at work will continue to preoccupy him. So at the end of each day, an executive may still be under some degree of stress, which will require 'treatment' if it is not to be allowed to get out of hand and develop into symptoms of stress. There are a number of possible ways of dealing with this day to day stress, and there can be no general prescription—what works for one executive will not help another. So the best idea is to try out a few of these suggestions and see which works best for you.

There is little doubt, though, that relaxation is crucial in combating stress. However, many executives find it hard to relax. The stresses of the working day often make it difficult to get in the right frame of mind for relaxation, which brings us back to earlier comments about the need for the right psychological attitude for following through health measures.

Far too many executives find that a large gin and tonic, or a whisky and soda, is an ideal way to wind down after a hard day at the office. Apart from the health risks of the alcohol itself (we shall discuss this in the following chapters) grabbing a nerve-settling drink as soon as the front door is shut, is a sure sign that an executive is on the road to a stress problem. Indeed, executives should see end-of-day drinking as a warning signal.

Instead of the glass of booze, or a slump in front of the TV, an executive needs to investigate other techniques of relaxation, if a permanent solution to day to day stress is to be found. A simple relaxation technique is one which is propounded by psychologists and therapists the world over. The first step involves sitting or lying down in a room which has no bright lights. It is preferable to be naked, although light clothing will not destroy the relaxation. You should be alone, and not able to be disturbed, so, if necessary, take the telephone off the hook, lock the bedroom door, and tell the family that you are not to be bothered for at least twenty minutes. The first few times you do this, the rest of the family might think you are going bonkers, but after a while they will probably accept it as part of the daily routine—they may even do it themselves once they've seen the improvement in your behaviour!

So, sitting or lying naked in a dimly lit, or darkened room, you are ready to begin. Concentrate on just one part of your body. It can be your left foot, your right elbow, it doesn't matter. Imagine that this part of your body is becoming warm, and heavy. Contract the muscles in that part of the body, and then relax them. Do this a few more times, then move on to another part of the body. Perform the same routine, and then repeat it again on another area of the body. Then move on to another part of the body, repeat the exercise, and so on until you have covered your whole body.

This should take about twenty minutes to half an hour, by which time you should feel much more relaxed, and less in need of an alcoholic drink. Performing this ritual on a nightly basis, not long after returning home from work, will help rid the tensions of the day, but like so many other things the time needed to do it can only be fitted in with good time management.

If this particular method of relaxation does not work for you, then there are alternatives. Yoga, for example, is a well-established method of relaxation. And there is medical evidence to support its use. Yoga is a combination of postural, breathing, and relaxation exercises, and according to research conducted by a British family doctor, Dr Chandra Patel, it can have positive health effects. Dr Patel has shown that yoga has a beneficial effect on blood pressure. Yoga can help control blood pressure and reduce the need for medicines to treat it. Apart from this measurable effect, many millions of people are agreed on the fact that yoga exercises increase their sense of calm, and help produce a relaxed feeling. Learning yoga exercises is not difficult. There are a number of books on the topic and there are many local clubs run by the Yoga for Health Foundation.

Going to yoga classes may not be some executives' ideal way of learning to relax. For these people there are even correspondence courses in relaxation techniques. These courses provide literature and cassette tapes with advice on how to relax.

However, relaxation sessions at home are fine for relieving end of the day tension, but many executives will suffer from acute periods of stress throughout the day. The additive effects of these 'attacks' of stress can lead to symptoms, so it is wise to attempt to control these in any stress-reduction programme.

Executives may become angry during heated discussions in meetings, they may become extremely tense if they are about to sack someone, or they may become acutely stressed if they are making major financial decisions. All of these stresses can mount up, adding to all of the other stressors, such as family problems, and so on. In addition, there are the stresses of travelling to and from work, which all increase the daily tension.

The way to cope with these acute stresses is first to deal with the attitude of mind. Think to yourself that the train might not be ten minutes late, yet again, because of inefficiency or sheer laziness; instead think that the driver is on the telephone receiving the good news that his wife has just given birth to a bouncing baby. Perhaps you could think that the traffic jam is not really due to the appalling government cutbacks on road spending, but rather due to the fact that we are so incredibly good at car manufacture. In other words, try to change your attitude of mind so that thoughts are more positive than usual. This is the first step in the battle against acutely stressful situations.

Next you have to deal with the body. The body's biological reaction to stress is to prepare for a fight or a hasty retreat from the stressful situation. This means that the muscles are primed for action, and the feelings of stress will only go away if and when the muscles are used. So, when faced with a stressful situation, remember that and use some muscles; clench and relax your fists every few seconds for about a minute. You can do this in meetings, with your hands below the table, or whilst standing talking to people with your hands behind your back. Take a couple of deep breaths at the same time and the feelings of tension will begin to go.

There are many situations during which these techniques for reducing acute stress can be utilized by executives. Many people go away on business, for example, sometimes to other parts of the world where time differences make it difficult to keep in touch with loved ones. This feeling of isolation from a spouse or a family can create feelings of tension, all of which contribute to the stress of the executive. One way out of this, which is relatively cheap—less than £100 ($160)—is to install a telephone answering machine at home. This can be used to keep in touch when international time zones would otherwise make it very difficult. Some executives on the move have telephones installed in their cars to keep in touch with everyone that matters, including their families. For many executives this expense may not be justified, but it does emphasize the fact that keeping in touch is an important technique for reducing worries that may lead to stress. You simply no longer have any uncertainty about situations if you can keep in touch. Uncertainty, as suggested earlier in this chapter, is one of the biggest causes of stress, and any technique which can be adopted to reduce levels of uncertainty can only be a bonus.

Sadly, though, many individuals are unable to control their stress. They go on and on striving for greater and greater success, working for longer and longer hours. These people feel that they are never achieving any goals they set and increasingly feel a failure. Eventually, they become isolated from their colleagues and feel more and more depressed. Then they find that they are unable to go on any longer. They just cannot cope. They have 'burnt out'.

Burnout

Burnout is the end point of stress for many executives. It is, literally, the psychological state of being at your wits end. You have totally collapsed, unable to give any more. This psychological collapse is a serious problem and happens in highly stressed individuals. It is very common in people who have singular jobs; people who are not part of a visible team, and upon whom many people depend. Burnout is particularly acute amongst the 'caring professions' such as medicine. The inability to control a chronic condition, for example, may be perceived by a carer as a failure on their part. Repeated feelings of failure help to compound the problem, only increasing the stresses and frustations and generally making the whole matter worse.

Any executive who has regular feelings of failure, or who thinks that goals and targets are not being adequately met, is probably at risk of burnout. The only sensible way to avoid the downhill slope towards the psychological collapse of burnout is to make every effort possible to achieve a healthy mind by the reduction of stress.

Summary

Nobody can achieve good health unless they put their mind to it. Any attempt to reduce the risks of disease has to begin with a change of mind to produce the will-power necessary to change a poor lifestyle. However, this positive attitude of a healthy mind is only possible if stress is controlled.

Stress is the response to outside stimuli which upset the status quo. The problem is different for all of us and no generalization can be made about the definition of stress, or its causes. Some possible causes are shown in Table 2 (see page 44). What can be said is that there are many common factors in people who have been under stress.

Stress leads to a cluster of physical symptoms and disorders. It is present in all walks of life, and it can be caused by pressures at work as well as problems at home. Stress cannot be isolated to work or home; it is produced as a result of a number of conflicting demands all of which lead to a feeling of uncertainty.

Combating stress can be performed if executives tackle the central issues of uncertainty. They need to manage their time effectively so as to be sure of what is to be done, by when, by whom, and so on. Executives need to reassess their home lives, devoting more time to spouses and children if necessary. A good sex life can be of particular help in reducing tensions in the home. Exercise is important in reducing stress since it produces feelings of relaxation, and has other important health spin-offs. A healthy diet should be adopted wherever possible—there is growing evidence that foods affect the way we think and behave. Relaxation is also important in dealing with the day to day pressures and problems. In addition, executives should take action to deal with the acute stresses of business life, thus reducing the additive effects of daily stressors, and increasing a calm attitude. Feelings of uncertainty can also be cut down if executives take steps to keep in touch with colleagues and loved ones, wherever they are.

Executive life does has its problems, but they are not

ones which are insurmountable. A programmed attack on stress, embarked upon with the right attitude of mind, can be effective in contributing to a healthy body and mind.

Table 2
SOME COMMON STRESS-INDUCING EVENTS

- Promotion
- Demotion
- Marriage
- Divorce
- Death of a close relative
- Moving house
- Changing job
- Threat of redundancy
- Repeated dissatisfaction with a job
- Illness in your children
- Starting or increasing a mortgage
- Trouble with the police
- Feeling unwell

If you answer 'Yes' to *any* of the following questions you should take care, since this suggest you may suffer from stress symptoms.

Table 3
STRESS QUESTIONNAIRE

- Do you work for more hours than the 'office day'?
- Do you regularly take work home with you?
- Do you ever need an alcoholic drink to help calm you down at the end of the working day?
- Do you ever drink alone?

- Do you wish you could spend more time with your family?

- Do you argue with your partner?

- Do you smoke to help relieve tension?

- Do you feel that you are always under-achieving your goals?

- Have you 'gone off' sex?

- Do you feel isolated from your colleagues?

The Healthy Mind Plan

- Answer the Stress Questionnaire in Table 3.

- Adopt a positive attitude of mind geared to dealing with your own health.

- Assess which areas of your life are causing stress and try to identify the particular stressors.

- Deal with any particular stressors which can be effectively dispensed with immediately.

- Begin an effective time management system, committing everything to writing.

- Look at your home life and make changes which will aid relaxation and reduce conflicts.

- Assess your sex life and rediscover the relaxing and rewarding value of sex.

- Begin a programme of exercise—three 20 minute sessions each week.

- Start to eat healthy foods. Choose hotels and restaurants which serve menus, offering 'healthy' foods.

- Perform a half-hour relaxation session at the end of each working day.

- Cut down the acute tensions of certain situations by exercising muscles.

- Reduce uncertainty by keeping in touch.

2
A Healthy Heart

In an average lifetime the human heart will beat for something like 2,500-3,000 million times. It works relentlessly from well before we are born for around seventy years, during which time it will have pumped some 48 million gallons (more than 218 million litres) of blood around. Only for a fraction of a second between each beat does the human heart have a chance to achieve anything approaching rest. Is it any wonder, then, that this constantly used organ is prone to disease? Remarkably, the human heart is extremely resilient, and treated with care and attention will give years of trouble-free service. Heart surgeons usually have to replace mechanical heart valves they insert into some patients every few years because they wear out. In most cases, human valves last a lifetime! This only goes to show the sheer efficiency and ability of the human heart.

It is therefore a sad reflection on our lifestyles, that heart disease is such a major cause of death. One in every five executives under the age of 64 will die of heart disease. In developed countries one death in every three is caused by heart disease. Diseases of the circulatory system, including the heart, account for just over half of all deaths.

Heart disease accounts for the loss of more than 60 million working days in the UK alone. Figures released by the British Heart Foundation reveal that a company with some 500 employees will lose around 3,000 working days each year because of heart disease—that is the equivalent to giving every employee an extra week's holiday. The costs to industry of a problem of this scale are enormous. The British Heart Foundation calculates that a company with 500 employees will lose almost £100,000 as a result of lost production due to heart disease in any given year.

The frightening statistics of heart disease go on. One man in every five who has a doctor's certificate to stay off work has received it as a result of heart disease. One person in every four who has a heart attack for the first time is dead within two hours of the start of the problem. Heart disease is the commonest cause of death in men between the ages of 35 and 64—it accounts for 45 deaths in every 100. Heart disease is not restricted to men. Women executives are also at risk. Heart disease is now the largest single cause of female deaths, accounting for one in every four deaths in women. Strokes, which are disturbances of blood supply to the brain, are the second commonest cause of death after heart disease, yet only one in three sufferers of a stroke die—the other two-thirds can become chronically disabled.

Whilst these statistics hold true for much of the developed world there are some notable exceptions. In Japan, for example, the biggest single killer is cancer, which causes almost half as many deaths again as heart diseases. However, the incidence of heart disease is rising in Japan. In the United States and Australia, on the other hand, rates of heart disease are falling, and according to figures released by the National Heart, Lung and Blood Advisory Council of the United States Department of Health and Human Sciences, heart and circulatory diseases declined by 26 per cent in the decade between 1968 and 1978. However, in 1981, cardiovascular diseases still accounted for some 50 per cent of all deaths in America, costing the nation some $80.5 billion. So, even though the United States is showing that it is succeeding in the battle against heart disease, it has yet to achieve a substantial reduction in the problem.

In the UK, however, heart disease statistics have changed very little in the last ten years. Despite attempts to encourage people to change their lifestyle so that their chances of heart disease are reduced, the message does not appear to have been carried across effectively, especially in the lower socio-economic groups.

Causes

The causes of these terrible statistics are varied. There is no one single cause of heart and circulatory disease. People who fall prey to these diseases do so as a result of a number of problems in combination.

There are three major factors which doctors claim to be at the root of cardiovascular disorders. These are—stress, diet, and smoking. People who are suffering from stress, or who have a poorly balanced diet, or who smoke, are all at an increased risk of suffering from heart and circulatory disease. People who are overweight also stand a much higher chance of suffering from heart disease, as do people who do not take regular exercise. There is also a genetic risk—as pointed out in Chapter 1, some people are born with a preponderance to a particular disease. Any executive who has parents, or other close relatives, who suffered from cardiovascular disease will tend to have a greater chance of falling prey to these illnesses too, and should therefore take extra precautions against the diseases.

Prevention

Because doctors have identified the major risk factors of heart and circulatory disease, they can produce logical advice on how to reduce the likelihood of becoming a sufferer. By reducing or removing the effects of these risk factors, the chances of heart disease become diminished. Although diet, stress, obesity, smoking, and lack of exercise are all accepted as risk factors, in actual fact there is one major problem which is to some extent dependent upon all of these other factors. This 'ultimate' risk factor is called 'atherosclerosis', and is the prime cause of heart and circulatory disease.

Atherosclerosis is the medical technical jargon for clogging up of the arteries. It happens when fatty deposits stick to the insides of the arteries, thus reducing the space available for the blood to travel. This increases the blood pressure, causing further damage to the blood vessels, and helping to produce blood clots which can lead to heart attacks or strokes. The blood vessels most prone to this sort of clogging up are the larger arteries throughout the body, those in the heart itself, and in the brain. If atherosclerosis develops in the blood vessels supplying the heart—the coronary arteries—then the blood supply to the area of the heart served by those arteries can become restricted, and can even lead to the death of this portion of the heart. This is a heart attack. If the arteries of the brain become clogged up, the blood supply to this vital organ can also be restricted leading to brain damage. Alternatively, the thickening of the artery as a result of atherosclerosis can cause it to burst as a result of too much pressure. This could cause a brain haemorrhage, for example. If arteries in the body become covered in layers of fat as a result of atherosclerosis the blood pressure of the cardiovascular system is raised, and that can lead to problems in itself—the higher the pressure, the harder the heart has to work, putting a strain upon its already heavy workload. High blood pressure too can help in the formation of atherosclerosis, so it just compounds the problem.

The fatty deposits which clog up the arteries in atherosclerosis contain a large amount of cholesterol. This is a chemical which is essential to life. It is used as an energy supply, in the manufacture of certain hormones and is also present in the membranes of the cells which make up our tissues. These tissues can manufacture their own cholesterol, but our diet provides the body with cholesterol too. After eating, any cholesterol is transported to the liver which converts it to bile acids, or stores it in special deposits in the liver itself. Sometimes the cholesterol itself is excreted, or even recirculated in our blood. It is this recirculating cholesterol which can be the start of atherosclerosis.

When the liver sends cholesterol around the body it does so by transporting the molecules of cholesterol on the back of other chemicals. Cholesterol itself is a fatty substance, and as such is not dissolvable in our bloodstream. Consequently it has to be transported in something which will dissolve. The principle is rather like using washing-up liquid to dissolve-off fatty deposits from a frying pan! The chemicals to which cholesterol is attached to allow it to go around our bodies are called 'lipoproteins'. The one which the liver uses to transport cholesterol is called 'low density lipoprotein' (LDL). Basically this is a chemical constructed of a fat and a protein, and as its name suggests, it is not very heavy. There is also another molecule involved in the passage of cholesterol around the body. This is called 'high density lipoprotein' (HDL) and is responsible for taking cholesterol from tissues back to the liver so that it can be broken down, stored, or excreted. In other words, it is taking cholesterol in the opposite direction to LDL.

It is this transportation of cholesterol around the body which can lead to atherosclerosis. Low density lipoprotein can be involved in a complex biochemical process which leads to the depositing of fats on artery walls. The chemical, LDL, also stimulates platelets—cells which aid blood clotting—to become more 'sticky', with the result that they become more likely to clump together in clots. These sticky clumps of platelets can become attached to the fatty deposits in the lining of the arteries, thus further decreasing the size of the available tube. There are other more complex factors involved in the formation of atherosclerosis, but the basic facts to remember are that high levels of cholesterol linked to LDL can be a trigger factor in the production of atherosclerosis and they can stimulate the formation of blood clots.

So any attempt at avoiding this major risk factor of atherosclerosis needs to aim at reducing the levels of LDL in the body. There is an added complication here: there is some evidence to suggest that the influence of LDL can be diminished if there are increased levels of HDL! High levels of HDL can actually keep down the amount of harmful LDL by reducing the levels of cholesterol available to it. But how do we go about reducing the levels of LDL, or increasing HDL? And where on earth do all the complicated, but accepted risk factors, such as diet and smoking, enter into this biochemical system?

The human body manufactures a considerable amount of cholesterol each day, roughly 1 gram of it. The average Western diet contains around 3 grams of cholesterol, about half of which is excreted in the faeces, and the remaining half remains in the liver for processing. But we don't really need all of this cholesterol which is retained in the liver. Should the body require more for any reason, it can, in most instances, simply step up the rate of manufacture. So one way to reduce the amount of LDL is to cut down on the amount of cholesterol in our diet. Less cholesterol taken into the system will reduce the availability of LDL, and so reduce the likelihood of atherosclerosis, which in turn lessens the chances of cardiovascular disease.

There are other influences on LDL and HDL levels. Stress, for example, increases LDL levels, as does smoking. Exercise, though, creates a rise in the beneficial HDL. In this way, the major risk factors that are commonly reported all influence atherosclerosis, which is a prime factor in the development of heart and circulatory disease. Interestingly, a female sex hormone, oestrogen, increases the level of the protective HDL, and this may be partly responsible for the fact that a lower percentage of female deaths are due to heart disease when compared to male deaths.

People without this narrowing of the arteries, or with only a small amount, do not have the same risks of heart disease as those people who do have atherosclerosis. So prevention of atherosclerosis must be the main aim of all executives wishing to reduce the already high risks of heart disease. This means they must reduce their levels of stress, decrease the amount of cholesterol in their diet, increase the amount of exercise they take and cut out smoking. At the same time they must ensure that their blood pressure remains as near normal as possible.

Stress

As the last chapter explained, stress can lead to a number of different physical complaints such as tiredness, low sex drive, poor appetite, dizziness, headaches and chest pain. However stress also leads to an upsurge in LDL levels, increasing the chances of cardiovascular complaints in addition to the problems associated with excess stress already discussed. On top of this, stress can also lead directly to heart disease.

When adrenalin is released in the fight or flight response, the body's natural reaction to a stressful situation, the heart is forced to pump more vigorously, so utilizing more oxygen. In some instances this could cause the oxygen supply to the heart muscle to become depleted, as it is using the oxygen at such a rapid rate. This in turn could lead to a heart attack in a susceptible individual. Some research has shown that as many as one in every five people who have been admitted to hospital after a heart attack have suffered some sort of emotional upset in the day leading up to the attack. There is evidence that certain types of people are particularly susceptible to stress-induced heart disease, which may result in these sudden, sometimes fatal, heart attacks.

These particularly prone individuals are classified as 'Type A' personalities. Type A is a term invented by two American heart specialists in the early 1960s. They noticed that there were two distinct types of people who visited their clinic. There were the alert, anxious, eager people and the rather 'laid-back' individuals. The doctors called the first group 'Type A' and the second group 'Type B'. Since this early definition of two basic behavioural types more research has been conducted and now there is a widely accepted definition of someone who exhibits Type A behaviour.

An individual who is a Type A person is usually ambitious, competitive, eager to achieve success, alert, and sometimes aggressive. In addition, someone who is a Type A person often speaks quickly, frequently feels there is not enough time to get things done, and will often have a tense facial expression (see Table 4). Many researchers have also found that this sort of behaviour pattern is worsened in a stressful environment.

Other research has demonstrated a sound biological basis for a link between Type A behaviour and heart disease. People who can be classified as Type A have been shown to have a much higher physiological response to stress than Type B people. The amount of adrenalin produced is higher, the demand on the heart is greater, and so on. This means that greater pressure is put upon a Type A individual's cardiovascular system, and it is therefore more prone to disease. The reasons are simple. The hormones produced in the fight or flight response to stress constrict the arteries, they make blood clotting more likely, and they affect the heartbeat itself. If a Type A person has other risks for a heart attack, such an executive may well eat the wrong kinds of foods for example, or smoke, then the reduced blood supply to the heart may well trigger off a heart attack. Alternatively, the behaviour-induced increase in blood clotting could cause a blockage of one of the arteries of the heart, also leading to a heart attack. Changes to the heart rhythm may also occur, and cause the heart to beat uncontrollably, resulting in death due to a lack of blood supply to the brain.

However, if you exhibit tendencies to Type A behaviour, do not despair. A heart attack is not inevitable, just more likely. Doctors and psychologists have demonstrated that people classified as Type A can be shown how to alter—without this change undermining their chances of being successful in their careers. Indeed, there are many successful Type B executives—the calm, considering business people, who never get in a fluster, and who infuriate Type As as a result!

If you answer 'Yes' to any of the following statements or questions then you exhibit some tendency towards Type A behaviour. The more positive responses you give, the more strongly Type A you are.

Table 4
ARE YOU A TYPE A PERSON?

- Meetings always seem to drag on too long at the office.

- You get annoyed when people are late for appointments.

- You always seem to be rushing from one meeting to another.

- You want to take over from your boss, as soon as possible.

- You are sometimes accused of shouting.

- Your secretary says that you speak too quickly on the dictating machine.

- You drive quickly.

- You sit on the edge of your seat in meetings.

- You write so quickly people find it difficult to read.

- You believe in 'looking after Number One'.

In one study in the United States, it was shown that people who had suffered a heart attack and who exhibited Type A tendencies had fewer second attacks after behaviour modification, compared to similar individuals who did not undergo the special training. It is worth noting that part of the behaviour modification recommended for Type A individuals was time management. This helped to reduce stress levels, as outlined in Chapter 1.

Stress also leads to atherosclerosis as a result of increases in cholesterol release from the liver. The hormonal changes involved in the fight or flight response cause cholesterol to be released into the bloodsteam. The biological purpose is to make available a ready energy supply should we have to run away from the stressful situation. However, repeated stress, either at home, at work, or both, can lead to a general increase in our circulating cholesterol levels, whether or not we are Type

A individuals. So even though Type A people are at the greatest risk of suffering from heart disease directly due to stress, it is possible for any individual to increase their likelihood of having cardiovascular problems because of repeated stress altering cholesterol levels. As we have seen, this directly affects the levels of low density lipoproteins in the bloodstream—the chemicals which begin the harmful process of atherosclerosis, or the clogging up of our arteries.

One point worth mentioning here is the presence of palpitations. Many people who have an emotional upset experience palpitations. Stress too can bring on this feeling of the heart beating. However, palpitations are not always serious. They may, though, be accompanied by pain in the chest, sweating, and dizziness, which indicates that the problem does need medical attention. Palpitations can also be caused by alcohol, so executives should remember this after a boozy lunch!

Another problem which can be confused with heart disease is also worth considering. Women executives, especially, may suffer from a psychological condition called 'panic disorder'. This is an emotional state of extreme panic, which is accompanied by chest pains, sweating, palpitations, and so on—all the signs of a heart attack. The condition is not serious, and can be treated both with psychological methods and with drugs. It is common, though. According to American psychiatrists something like 5 per cent of the population suffers from panic disorder, and two-thirds of these are women. In fact, the psychological effects of our brain on our heart are so complex that it has been suggested that one person in every seven who visits a heart specialist because of an apparent cardiovascular disorder is eventually referred to a psychiatrist because all of the tests performed find nothing wrong with the heart!

However, this does not mean that executives should not be warned by apparent heart symptoms, or take them lightly. Any disturbances or symptoms should be reported to a doctor for investigation, and consideration should be given to behaviour modification so that the effects of stress can be lessened. Following the plan of Chapter 1 should help reduce the risks of heart disease imposed by excess stress.

However, people who exhibit gross tendencies towards Type A behaviour may need more practical and individual help. For these people advice and therapy can be obtained from specialist organizations, such as the UK's Executive Health Screening. This is an organization which offers a nationwide network of counsellors, doctors, psychiatrists, psychologists, and therapists for a wide variety of companies. Firms can use Executive Health Screening to help them decide on the suitability of applicants for the job—a 900-question computer test helps weed out those people who may become too stressed in particular situations.

However, Executive Health Screening also provides individual help and advice to people who may be under stress, or who are aware than they could suffer from stress and need to be taught how to avoid it. There are other similar facilities to Executive Health Screening, and they are being increasingly used by companies as the economic costs of stress, and heart disease, are becoming apparent. However, stress is not the only cause of changes to the cardiovascular system, and therefore a higher risk of heart disease.

Diet

It will come as no surprise to learn that the food we eat and the drink we consume can have a profound effect upon LDL and cholesterol, and consequently on the health of the circulatory system as a whole. Food consists of a number of basic constituents, namely, protein, carbohydrate, fats, fibre, water, vitamins, minerals, individual chemicals found in tiny amounts (trace elements), and additives. These components of food provide us with energy, warmth and the necessary chemicals to manufacture the molecules our bodies need for survival.

Proteins are required to repair and construct our tissues, and are also used as an energy store after having been converted to fat. Carbohydrates are our main supply of energy. Fats too are a supply of energy, and together with carbohydrates they supply a total of 90 per cent of our daily energy requirement. Fats contain cholesterol. Fibre is non-digestible, but is a necessary part of our diet since it enables the easier movement of foods through our digestive tract.

Vitamins, minerals, and trace elements are all required in small amounts to help the body manufacture certain chemicals, such as the haemoglobin in our blood which carries oxygen around. The vast majority of food additives have no biological requirement, and are generally only included in foods to help preserve them, alter their appearance, and enhance their flavour.

All of these foods can together influence heart disease in a very simple fashion. If we eat too much food in general we become fat, and obesity is clearly linked to heart disease. Obesity should not be thought of as being grossly overweight. Correctly used, the word obese means that the person described has stored extra fats to make them merely 10 per cent over their ideal weight. This means if someone who should weigh around 12 stones (168lbs, 76.3kg) puts on weight and becomes just over 13 stones (185lb, 84kg) they will be technically obese, even though they might not look 'fat'. Tables of ideal heights and weight of men and women of different body builds have been developed over the years, largely by life assurance firms and actuaries. These tables show the ideal weight of someone of a given height. Doctors agree that we should all stay within 10 per cent of our ideal weight if we are to remain free of the risks imposed by obesity. You can check your weight using Table 5 (see pages 59 and 60).

We can remain within these general weight limits providing we eat the right amount of food for the energy requirements of our bodies. It is a simple equation: input should equal output. Any excess input will be a profit for the body registered as stored fat, and an increase in overall weight. According to the Department of Health and Social

Table 5
RECOMMENDED WEIGHTS IN RELATION TO HEIGHT

	Height without shoes		Recommended Average weight without clothes		Weight Range	
MEN	Inches	Cms	Pounds	Kgs	Pounds	Kgs
	62	158	123	56	112-141	51-64
	63	160	127	58	115-144	52-65
	64	163	130	59	118-148	54-67
	65	165	133	60	121-152	55-69
	66	168	136	62	124-156	56-71
	67	170	140	64	128-161	58-73
	68	173	145	66	132-166	60-75
	69	175	149	68	136-170	62-77
	70	178	153	70	140-174	64-79
	71	180	158	72	144-179	65-81
	72	183	162	74	148-184	67-84
	73	185	166	76	152-189	69-86
	74	188	171	78	156-194	71-88
	75	191	176	80	160-199	73-90
	76	193	181	82	164-204	74-92
WOMEN	Inches	Cms	Pounds	Kgs	Pounds	Kgs
	58	147	102	46	92-119	42-54
	59	150	104	47	94-122	43-55
	60	152	107	48	96-125	44-57
	61	155	110	50	99-128	45-58
	62	158	113	51	102-131	46-59
	63	160	116	53	105-134	48-61
	64	163	120	54	108-138	49-63
	65	165	123	56	111-142	50-64
	66	168	128	58	114-146	52-66
	67	170	132	60	118-150	54-68
	68	173	136	62	122-154	55-70
	69	175	140	64	126-158	57-72
	70	178	144	65	130-163	59-74
	71	180	148	67	134-168	61-76
	72	183	152	69	138-173	63-78

(Table reproduced from 'The Facts About Obesity', with permission from BUPA).

Security in the UK men in sedentary occupations, such as office work, need 60g of protein each day, and women will need about 54g of protein each day. The figure is slightly higher for men under the age of 35, who will require some 62g of protein each day.

The DHSS then recommends a daily total allowance of Calories, which are a measure of the energy provided by everything we eat, but principally of fats and carbohydrates. A Calorie should not be confused with a calorie. A Calorie represents 1,000 calories. For the sake of avoiding confusion, Calories are frequently referred to as 'kilocalories', or 'kcal', and they shall be mentioned in this manner throughout the rest of this book.

All our foods and drinks can be measured and the number of kilocalories they provide calculated in a laboratory. In order to provide the amount of energy required for a day's work the average male executive requires 2,500 kilocalories each day. A female executive requires less, around 2,100 kilocalories. As we get older we also require fewer kilocalories, so male executives past middle-age will be able to meet their energy needs with only 2,400 kilocalories, and women can drop their requirements to 1,900 kilocalories. A food intake which leads to greater amounts than these on a regular basis will lead to an increase in weight. It is acceptable to have extra kilocalories occasionally, but it is the regular overeating which will lead to obesity, quickly. The energy provided in an average sized apple, for example, requires a 12 minute walk to be disposed of. Think then of the daily excesses to which many executives have grown accustomed—regular business lunches, three course meals in hotels, and so on—and it is easy to understand how feasible it is for executives to become obese.

Obesity—just a 10 per cent increase in ideal weight, remember—is harmful. People who are overweight tend to die younger than those people who are within the 10 per cent limit above their ideal weight. Obese people also tend to suffer more from heart disease as a result of an increase in blood pressure. Excess body weight creates pressure on the circulatory system and causes a generalized increase in blood pressure.

As has already been explained this is linked to heart disease, and also, more strongly, to strokes—the two biggest killers in the developed world. The likelihood of suffering from these problems can only be prevented if obesity is avoided by taking in the right amount of kilocalories, which for most of us means eating less. Obesity is also linked to a number of other disorders, such as diabetes, and certain types of cancer, such as cancer of the bowel. These problems will be discussed in detail in the next chapter.

The food we eat, however, does not contribute to our risk of cardiovascular disease simply by increasing our weight and so our blood pressure—which is bad enough in itself. Fats, which provide about 40 per cent of our energy supply, also contain cholesterol. This has already been described as being a major influential factor in the development of atherosclerosis, the prime cause of heart disease. The extra cholesterol we eat can, obviously, increase the amount of the chemical and its associated low density lipoprotein circulating in our bloodstream. However, even if we removed all of the cholesterol from our diets experts agree that the reduction in our circulating cholesterol level would only be around 10 to 15 per cent. For people who already have high levels of LDL and cholesterol in their bloodstream as a result of stress, smoking, and so on, this reduction, although helpful, would not make much impact. In addition, some cholesterol in our diet is probably necessary.

Far more important in the cholesterol and diet story is the fat itself. Basically, there are two types of fats in foods. These are called 'saturated' and 'unsaturated', terms which come from basic chemistry: a saturated fat is one which is chemically complete and has no space in its molecule for other atoms; unsaturated fats do have spaces available for other atoms, which are not taken up. If there is just one space it is called a 'monounsaturated fat', but if there is space for more than one extra atom it is called a 'polyunsaturated fat'.

There is considerable evidence that these fats affect the levels of cholesterol and lipoproteins in our bloodstream.

Consequently, eating these fats can affect the formation of atherosclerosis, and hence our risk of heart and circulatory disease. Basically, saturated fats are the baddies, whilst polyunsaturated fats are beneficial. The reason is the different effects these two types of fats have on our lipoprotein levels.

A variety of research studies have shown that, in general, saturated fats increase the absorption of cholesterol from our diet, and also increase the body's production of cholesterol, mainly in the liver. Conversely, polyunsaturated fats reduce the amount of cholesterol absorbed by the food we eat, promote its excretion in our faeces, and reduce the amount pumped into the blood-steam by our liver. Consequently, saturated fats increase the amount of cholesterol, and associated LDL, in our bloodstream, whilst polyunsaturated fats reduce the levels of these atherosclerosis-inducing chemicals. So, in order to prevent heart disease it is important to ensure that the balance of fats we eat is tipped towards the polyunsaturated fat side of the scale, rather than towards saturated fats.

A panel of experts convened by the United States National Heart, Lung and Blood Institute met in 1984 to look into the whole debate about cholesterol and heart disease. That panel's report says that lowering the levels of cholesterol in the blood 'definitely' reduces the risk of a heart attack.

The Institute's recommendations were that every American, except young children, should cut down their total intake of fat so that it represented only 30 per cent of the kilocalorie requirement, compared to the normal average level of 40 per cent. The Institute also recommended that one-third of this fat should be the polyunsaturated kind, and less than one-third should be saturated.

In other words, the message from American experts was the same as that from the UK Government's Committee on Medical Aspects of Food Policy (COMA), which also published its report on 'Diet and Cardiovascular Disease' in 1984. That message was simple: eat less fats, and change the proportion of those fats so that there is more polyunsaturated fat in the diet than saturated fat.

In Japan, as mentioned earlier, the incidence of heart disease is lower than that of the UK or the US. The Japanese diet is traditionally lower in fat, especially saturated fats. However, coincidentally with an increased acceptance of 'American' or 'European' diets, there has been a rise in the level of heart disease. This has provided further circumstantial evidence for a link between diet and heart disease.

Some fats are what is known as 'essential'. They cannot be manufactured by the body and must be taken in our diet. One of these is called linoleic acid, which is used to produce a chemical called thromboxane A_2, which is used in the clotting of blood. If we eat too much linoleic acid we could be unnecessarily increasing the 'stickiness' of our blood, making it more likely to clot, and therefore more able to clog up those vital arteries which supply the heart. However, fortunately, another acid, called eicosapentaenoic acid, EPA for short, inhibits this effect.

Research has shown that people who have diets rich in EPA, such as eskimos who eat a lot of fish, have significantly lower rates of heart disease when compared to people who do not eat so much EPA. In addition, groups of people who have been given pills containing EPA have been shown to benefit because their blood clotting cells, platelets, become less 'sticky', and are therefore less likely to contribute to the formation of heart disease inducing clots.

However, there are other dietary considerations which need to be taken into account if people wish to prevent heart and circulatory disease. Research in Norway, for example, has shown that drinking coffee pushes up the level of cholesterol in the bloodstream. Scientists from the Arctic fishing town of Tromsø found that blood cholesterol levels were reduced in people who gave up drinking coffee for ten weeks, compared to others who carried on drinking coffee. Returning to drinking coffee put the cholesterol levels back up in those people who had abstained, but filtered coffee did not produce this effect.

Other studies have implicated sugar in the development of heart disease. Some tribes in Africa, for example, eat relatively high levels of fats but do not have sugar. These tribes have a lower recorded incidence of heart disease than thoses tribes who add sugar to their diet. Cholesterol levels have also been shown to be lower in people who do not eat sugar.

Fibre is another part of our diet which can influence heart disease. There is growing evidence that those people who eat a diet rich in fibre, such as vegetarians, suffer a lower incidence of heart disease than those people who have lower intakes of fibre.

Salt has also entered the debate about heart disease. Doctors are still arguing about the precise role of salt in the production of high blood pressure. However, what is clear from studies so far, is that those people who have high blood pressure are helped by a low salt diet. Their blood pressure drops as a result of the diet, and consequently this helps in reducing their risk of heart and circulatory disease.

Taking all these factors into account, the likelihood of heart disease can be drastically reduced with alterations in diet. Basically, these alterations should ensure that we eat the recommended daily allowance of protein, as suggested by the UK's DHSS; that we eat fewer fats, but that we should eat a greater proportion of polyunsaturated fats; that the amount of fibre we eat is increased; that people with high blood pressure eat less salt; and that the amount of food containing EPA, such as fish, is increased. In addition it is probably a good idea to eat less sugar too. Not only will this help your heart, it will benefit your teeth as well. If we can achieve this sort of change to our daily diet then there is substantial evidence to suggest that the risk of atherosclerosis, and therefore of heart and circulatory disease, is reduced. This reduction in risk is also greatest for those individuals already at higher than average likelihood of suffering from these conditions. However, despite everything that has been said thus far in this chapter, those people who are at the greatest risk of developing heart disease are those executives who smoke.

Smoking

Without doubt smoking is the biggest single cause of ill-health in the Western world. It is almost certainly behind more 'early' deaths than any other activity in our lives today. Smoking is responsible for at least 50,000 'early' deaths each year in the UK.

This is the number of people whose lives have been curtailed directly as a result of smoking. In addition, there are thought to be many other deaths where smoking has been a major contributory factor. Smoking is also a major cause of some chronic disorders, such as bronchitis, which can be severely disabling. Smoking too is also one of the most significant precursors to the need for amputation since it can damage the blood supply to the limbs.

In 1962 the Royal College of Physicians of England published a classic document called 'Smoking and Health'. This detailed the serious risks of smoking, the main one being lung cancer. Two years later the Surgeon General in the United States published another report with the same title. Together, these two major publications drew the world attention to the dangers of smoking, and people began to realize that smoking could cause lung cancer. It began to put people off smoking.

In 1959 the Institute of Directors examined the habits of its members. Their survey revealed that 70 per cent of the membership of the Institute smoked (*Ease and Disease*, Beric Wright, Longman 1986). Today, smokers form about 35 per cent of the population. Statistics also reveal that professionals, the sorts of people who may be members of the Institute, also smoke less than average.

However, various surveys over the years have revealed that the majority of people do not realize that smoking is linked to heart and circulatory disorders. The lung cancer story does seem to have been well understood, but the fact that smoking causes cardiovascular disease is something which many people still do not realize. In fact a smoker is more likely to suffer from cardiovascular disease than lung cancer.

One in every three coronary heart attacks has been

attributed directly to smoking; research in Finland has shown that sufferers of heart attacks who have smoked are almost twice as likely to die than similar people who have not smoked. A Swedish study has revealed that 52 per cent of 'excess' deaths—the number of people dying above the average for a given age-range and sex—are from cardiovascular disease caused by smoking; lung cancer only accounts for 19 per cent of the excess deaths.

Consequently, it is clear that the greatest risk of smoking is in the development of cardiovascular disease, and not lung cancer. Sadly, this message is not being promoted anywhere near hard enough.

Many health warnings on cigarette advertisements do not point out the most serious danger of smoking, cardiovascular disease. Neither do these sorts of warnings emphasize the fact that repeated studies have shown that the risks of suffering from cardiovascular trouble as a result of smoking are greatest in those people who already have other risk factors, such as a poor diet, stress, Type A behaviour, and so on. Yet it is executives under stress who may be more likely to smoke to relieve the tension.

But how does smoking affect the cardiovascular system in such a fatally damaging way? Smoking has its effects in a number of different ways. Firstly, it directly raises the levels of low density lipoprotein circulating in the bloodstream. As has already been demonstrated this is the major risk factor in the development of circulatory disease, and is the prime cause of heart attacks. In addition smoking also mimics the fight or flight response: it triggers an increase in adrenalin release. This, in itself, helps increase LDL levels, but it also makes the heart pump faster. If the cardiovascular system is already under strain as a result of atherosclerosis, then the work of the heart becomes difficult, and a fatal heart attack can result.

In addition, the inhaled smoke contains carbon monoxide, which can combine with haemoglobin, the chemial which transports oxygen in the bloodstream. Most smokers have something like 5 per cent of their haemoglobin stolen by carbon monoxide in this way. So, the availability of oxygen can be reduced, further putting a strain on the heart and the circulatory system. Carbon monoxide in the blood has also been linked with an increase in atherosclerosis, putting an additional strain on the entire circulatory system. Smoking can also reduce the levels of oestrogen in women. As has already been explained, this hormone does provide some degree of protection for women against cardiovascular problems. The only way out of this situation is to give up smoking completely.

Many people have believed that reducing the number of cigarettes they smoke, or by smoking low tar brands, or by transferring to cigars or a pipe, they can cut down the risks of disease. The world's largest on-going study of heart disease has been conducted in Framingham, Massachusetts, and is called 'The Framingham Study'. This research has found that the fewer cigarettes smoked the lower the risk of heart disease. This 'dose-response', though, may have been misinterpreted. The Framingham Study showed that even though people who smoked less than 20 cigarettes each day had a lower risk of heart disease than those people who smoked 20 or more cigarettes a day, they still had *double* the risk of heart disease of people who had given up smoking. Low tar cigarettes may also not be of much help in reducing the risks. Cigarettes contain nicotine which is an addictive drug, and often people who switch to low tar brands try to make up for the lower amount of nicotine by smoking more cigarettes, as well as by inhaling more deeply.

The idea that switching from cigarettes to a pipe or cigar will be less harmful may also be a false notion. People who start smoking cigars or pipes will not usually inhale the more distasteful smoke, but people who have smoked cigarettes previously will probably do so. Consequently, they will continue to put their lives at risk, and in addition, pipe smoking is linked more strongly with cancers of the mouth and tongue. So, there is only one real way to cut the risks of smoking and prevent heart disease—stop smoking altogether.

Some critics suggest that there is little evidence to support the notion that stopping smoking is an effective way of reducing the health risks. They claim that 'the damage is done now, so why give up?' Some studies have been used to back these sorts of claims, showing that giving up cigarettes did not reduce the risks of heart disease back to that of the non-smoker for something like 15 years. However, new research from Boston University School of Medicine shows that the risks of smoking are dramatically reduced after giving up. Research conducted there in 1985 showed that if people gave up smoking, their risk of suffering from coronary heart disease was equal to that of a non-smoker within two years of quitting the habit.

Smoking amongst executives is, fortunately, at a lower level than that of the Western population as a whole. However, up to one in three executives smoke, and are consequently putting their own lives at risk. In addition, they are putting the lives of their colleagues, and their families at risk too. The World Health Organization has claimed that 'passive smoking'—the involuntary inhalation of smoke that some inconsiderate smoker is puffing all over the room—is an 'indisputable health risk'. Passive smoking has also been shown by Danish scientists to be a risk to babies still in the womb by possibly causing a reduction in their birthweight—a factor which is a key to their survival. Consequently, executives who smoke could be damaging the unborn babies of women who work in the same office, and perhaps also their own child being carried by their wife.

The only real preventative measure for reducing all the risks associated with smoking is to give up, or preferably never smoke at all. However, the passive smoking issue is a controversial one, and many executives will be forced into passive smoking when they visit public houses, bars, restaurants, and so on. This brings us to another major risk factor in the development of heart disease—alcohol.

Alcohol

Alcohol is clearly linked to the development of specific

cardiovascular problems and in high doses can cause damage to the heart itself.

Executive life frequently revolves around alcohol; there are the lunchtime meetings in restaurants and hotels, the nights away alone in strange cities, the cocktail receptions, and the end of day 'quick one' with the lads. Alcoholic drinks are an accepted part of the culture of the executive world. Yet alcohol is responsible for some 14 million working days lost each year in the UK alone. Many people know of the severe, often fatal, damage which alcohol can wreak upon the liver (this will be discussed in the next chapter), but not everyone is aware of the link between heart disease and alcohol. It is now known that alcohol raises the level of fats in the bloodstream, and that it can alter the regularity of the natural heartbeat, as well as interfering directly with the cells of the heart itself—all of which greatly increase the risk of heart disease.

Someone who has four or more glasses of wine (or equivalent) each day, as many executives may well do, is *twice* as likely to die of heart disease than a non-drinker. Alcohol increases blood pressure, and regular drinking can contribute to a permanently raised blood pressure, which, as has already been seen, can further increase the risks of heart and circulatory disease. In addition, alcohol can directly cause a heart attack if it is drunk in excess. Executives who go away on conferences may well enter into a 'binge' of alcoholic excesses and could therefore be risking a heart attack. The physiological reason for this problem is not yet fully understood.

Some researchers have shown that small smounts of alcohol, however, may actually prevent a heart attack. Something like a couple of glasses of wine a day, or say 1 pint of beer, has been shown to raise the levels of the protective, beneficial, high density lipoprotein in the bloodstream. These sorts of claims are controversial. The main problem appears to be in dispensing such advice to all and sundry. Whilst this fact may be true, and has yet to be proven, sticking to one or two glasses a day would be difficult for many people. Regular drinking of any amount could be a temptation for more, which could be harmful.

There are two possibilities to prevent heart disease as a result of alcohol. The first is to abstain from taking this addictive drug altogether. However, this is a rather 'killjoy' attitude, and the damage which is performed by just one alcoholic drink is generally repaired fairly quickly by the body itself. The second means of preventing heart disease due to alcohol is by controlling your drinking. According to recent psychological evidence, it seems that controlled drinking is the most appropriate method of dealing with alcohol-related illness. By controlling your alcohol intake you are able to enjoy yourelf, and not appear 'unusual' at parties and so on, yet are able to consciously limit the amount you drink to sensible levels.

Sadly, though, many executives do not control their alcohol intake. Not only is alcohol an accepted part of the executive world, but people who work in this world tend to have greater disposable incomes and are therefore able to afford more drink. The company expense account is also another reason for high levels of alcohol consumption. There is a real need for improved education about the effects of alcohol on the heart, and thankfully organizations such as 'Alcohol Concern' have instituted a programme in a 'Work Advisory Service' to do just that. Indeed, Alcohol Concern is encouraging bosses to produce their own company alcohol policies so that employees can learn to drink sensibly. Since drinking loses industry so many productive working days, such an idea seems economically sensible to firms as well as being a major contribution to the reduction of heart disease risks amongst executives.

The executive heart

So we have seen how various factors influence the likelihood of heart and circulatory disease, but how do all of these things intertwine to produce their effects in executives?

Whilst it is difficult to generalize about people working in executive positions, it is likely that they will be ambitious. They are therefore more likely to exhibit tendencies to Type A behaviour, thus increasing their heart disease risk. They frequently eat large 'business lunches' or meals in hotels. Alcohol is an accepted part of the executive culture, and smoking may be a way of reducing the pressures of some of the work. In addition, the financial health of executives may be a contributory factor to their waistline! People who have plenty of disposable income tend to eat more than they should, and consequently their obesity is also increasing their risk of heart disease.

As has already been stated, the prime cause of heart and circulatory disease is a condition known as atherosclerosis—the clogging up of our arteries. The reasons for this happening are varied, but executive life seems to have all of them—diet, smoking, alcohol, obesity, and stress.

Reducing the risks

The key to cutting down the risk of heart disease is to avoid atherosclerosis. As already explained this means reducing stress, changing from Type A behaviour, giving up smoking, drinking sensibly, maintaining an ideal weight, and eating a healthy diet. In addition, there is strong, solid evidence, which shows that regular exercise can reduce the levels of low density lipoproteins in the blood, and increase the beneficial HDL, thus providing an additional bonus in attempts to reduce atherosclerosis. One study showed that out of a group of men who exercised, there were fewer cases of heart disease compared to a group who did no exercise.

But the executive lifestyle does not always provide the time, or foster the inclination to do all of these things. Or does it? Take smoking, for example. Many more executives are non-smokers than smokers. These non-smokers may well be concerned about the amount of 'passive smoking' to which they are subject in their working life. As we have already seen, passive smoking is declared a health risk by the World Health Organization, but executives may find themselves in meetings where a colleague is smoking, or in hotels where other guests are smoking. There are ways out of this, however. Because there are more executives who do not smoke it would be easy to obtain support for a total ban on smoking in meetings, or in certain areas of the building, for example, in 'reception'. Many companies do this, and restrict smokers to their own office if they wish to indulge.

Hotels too are coming round to the idea of no-smoking areas. For example, Crest Hotels pioneered the idea of no-smoking bedrooms, only available to non-smokers. Consequently, there is no lingering musty smoky smell in these rooms and no lurking particles of smoke to be breathed in. Crest has also introduced no-smoking areas in its restaurants and in its public rooms. Trust House Forte too has no-smoking bedrooms and no-smoking public areas, as have Inter-Continental Hotels, and Stakis Hotels. No-smoking bedrooms can also be found in Sheraton Hotels and Embassy Hotels, amongst others. Executives wishing to avoid the effects of inhaling too much of a polluted atmosphere should really book into a hotel of one of these chains, or any of the other hotels which provide no-smoking rooms and areas. When booking a room, why not ask if such facilities are provided, and if not go to a hotel where they are? Hoteliers will soon get the message; in researching this book it was discovered than an average of 50 per cent of hotel business comes from business men and women and, in the UK, spending at least around £150 to £250 each time they stay. So pressure from executives can achieve a change in the direction of providing more facilities for the majority—non-smokers.

Hotels are also increasingly recognizing the value of exercise and fitness. Many hotels now have gymnasia, swimming pools, and other types of fitness centres. Others, who do not have these facilities frequently have a link-up with a local gym so that guests can visit these free of charge, or for a modest fee. Other hotels have devised 'jogging maps' around parks and city centres. Executives who have started a fitness programme should not think that by going away from home that their programme need be interrupted. Choosing the hotel that provides fitness facilities is all that is needed. As stated in the previous chapter, one hour's worth of exercise each week is all that is recommended to improve health, so going away for a couple of days means that you do not have to find a hotel which provides the full range of facilities. A pool, or ample countryside for long walks, is all that is needed.

Staying in hotels, though, can be a temptation for the stomach. Hotel restaurants are notoriously good. Sadly, many examples of excellent cuisine, such as that provided in the finest hotels, are also examples of the sorts of foods you should avoid if you wish to cut down the risks of developing atherosclerosis. Nowadays, there are hotels which have 'healthy menus' and it would be wise to choose one of these. If however this is not possible there are some basic tips about choosing foods from menus which should be remembered.

Protein is a daily requirement. Foods that provide large amounts of protein include meat, fish, and poultry. These are almost certain to appear on most hotel menus. However, red meat is the one protein-containing food that is likely to provide an increased risk of atherosclerosis. Whilst red meat, on occasion, is unlikely to be harmful, regular eating of large amounts of red meat may be a contributor to an increased risk of heart disease. Indeed, many experts now believe that red meat should only be eaten in about two meals each week. So choose fish, or poultry, or a vegetarian meal.

Try to avoid anything with extremely rich sauces, especially if you already have a higher than average risk of heart disease, for example if you smoke. Choose a meal that has plenty of fibre; fresh vegetables help, and if offered a bread roll take a wholemeal one, for example.

When choosing sweets, avoid repeatedly eating fat-laden foods such as cheese or gateaux. Try the fresh fruit salad, or a piece of fruit—that has plenty of fibre. And avoid lashings of cream. It is nice, admittedly, and is perfectly acceptable from time to time, but it is the repeated eating of these atherosclerosis-inducing foods that will do the damage, especially for executives at risk of heart disease. The answer is to try and achieve a balance in all of the things you eat. Executives who stay regularly in hotels can do this, simply by taking an extra minute or two whilst looking at the menu. Don't just quickly opt for the steak and chips. What about the Dover Sole with a baked potato?

Another difficulty with hotels is the bar! Executives tend to stay in hotels either alone, or in large groups such as at a sales meeting, or at a conference. Either occasion can lead to excess alcohol consumption. The executive alone finds that sitting in the bar having a quiet chat with the bar tender, or other guests is a much more pleasant way of passing the evening than sitting in the bedroom reading. An executive who is at a sales meeting or conference would feel expected to join in the jollity at the bar, after all 'everyone' is there and 'I would feel silly if I said I wanted to stay in my room to read'!!

The answer to this problem is to learn the rules about controlled drinking. Alcohol in small amounts, on an irregular basis, seems unlikely to cause permanent damage in the vast majority of people. So executives staying in hotels need not deprive themselves of booze altogether. Controlled drinking will allow an executive to drink, and still feel a part of any *bonhomie* at a conference, yet will help prevent any health damage.

For example, choose drinks which require time to drink. Whilst a pint of beer will contain roughly the same amount of alcohol as a large gin and tonic, it takes most people considerably longer to drink. So in a given space of time it is possible to drink more shorts, than pints of beer, consequently increasing the overall alcohol intake.

Some people, though, do not like drinking pints of beer or lager. Some women executives may feel that they look silly drinking a pint, though quite why this should be so remains a mystery. Some people prefer short drinks, they like the taste of gin, or whisky, for example. If you are like this then there are ways to ensure that you keep the amount of alcohol down. Always use a mixer—add plenty of tonic to gin, use ginger ale, or water with whisky, add orange juice to vodka, for example. These mixers add to the volume of the drink making you take more time to drink them thus reducing the potential amount of alcohol drinkable. In addition, they help fill up the stomach, making you want less anyway.

There are also alternatives to these sorts of steps. A wide range of 'low alcohol' beverages are now becoming available and are stocked in many hotels. These taste roughly the same as traditional alcoholic drinks, and contain only a tiny percentage of alcohol. These can be drunk instead of alcoholic drinks, or between stronger drinks to help reduce the overall alcohol intake. Many hotel barmen are expert cocktail makers and know a wide range of non-alcoholic drinks made from fruit juices and minerals. Asking the hotel barman for one of these is a good idea, and no one will know that you are not drinking alcohol if that worries you. Remember too, for example, that carbonated mineral water looks identical to gin and tonic and you will not feel isolated if you drink this, as many people might do if they were drinking orange juice amongst a crowd of gin-swillers.

When in an hotel, especially with other executives, it is a good idea to start any evening which could end up with plenty of alcohol flowing with a large soft drink, such as a large glass of lemonade. This will quench your thirst, help fill up the stomach, and reduce your need to throw back glass after glass of the damaging alcohol-containing drinks. Like eating, drinking is something which only requires a moment or two of extra thought to be able to do it sensibly and with a reduced risk of heart disease. These sorts of tips are also useful for end of day drinking, although the need for that can be reduced by appropriate stress control.

Stress is an important factor in the development of heart disease. Executive life can induce stress, and in order to cut down on the chances of having heart trouble business men and women alike need to reduce their stress levels. Fortunately, the tips for reducing heart disease in general, such as a healthy diet, exercise, and so on are also valuable in the reduction of stress. But a key to the stress question is to reduce the level of uncertainty in life. Planning and careful time management are important aspects of making things more certain. So too is a keen eye on home life, making sure that it is not in conflict with work. Careful management of time will allow this, but it will also free hours for another aspect of reducing the risks of heart disease—exercise.

Executives can exercise, despite complaints that facilities are not available and so on. More and more companies are realizing the benefits of exercise and office-based fitness suites are being built by the day. The use of these will benefit all executives, but no one should engage upon a programme of fitness training without the approval of a medical practitioner. This is especially true for people who have rarely exercised before. For these people the best exercise to start with is walking. After checking with a doctor, take a walk for half an hour three times a week. Doing this after work will also help reduce the tensions of the day. Once walking becomes easy, then it is possible to go on to jogging, or swimming, or to fitness training in a gym.

However do not enter into any of these activities without the advice of your doctor. A medical practitioner will be able to check that your system is up to the strain of increased exercise. Exercise itself can increase the risk of heart disease in those people who are susceptible, and who are already at an increased risk of trouble, such as the obese. Consulting a doctor will ensure that a measured programme can take place, and that the risks of atherosclerosis can be reduced. Another important thing to remember in any exercise programme is always to do a few warm-up exercises before starting. These should involve gentle bending and stretching movements of the limbs, the neck, and the body, in order to loosen up the muscles and improve the circulation. Launching straight in to vigorous exercise will not help, but the warm-ups will improve the blood flow to the muscles making them better able to respond to the full fitness programme.

Executives, though they may manage their time effectively, may well complain that finding time for exercise programmes can still be difficult. For these executives it is important to obtain as much muscular movement as possible during the day—use stairs instead of lifts, walk to a lunch appointment instead of taking a taxi and so on.

Summary

Diseases of the heart and of the cardiovascular system are most likely in those people who have a condition known as atherosclerosis, which is a clogging up of the arteries. This clogging up restricts the movement of blood and puts an extra strain on the heart, making it more vulnerable to trouble.

This atherosclerosis is largely due to an excess of chemicals called low density lipoproteins which are used to transport cholesterol around the body. A number of different factors affect the levels of low density lipoproteins and can interact to increase the likelihood of heart disease in any given individual. Firstly, the process of atherosclerosis is affected by diet. A diet which is low in cholesterol and is low in fat will help lessen the chances of atherosclerosis developing. Obesity is also linked to an increase in the problem of atherosclerosis, and also contributes to the chances of heart disease by increasing blood pressure. Smoking also seriously affects the process of atherosclerosis and additionally reduces the availability of oxygen in the blood, thus worsening an already poor situation. Smoking can be particularly harmful for a woman's heart since it removes the effect of female hormones which do provide a degree of protection by inhibiting the development of too much atherosclerosis.

Another factor in the development of heart and circulatory disorders is stress and Type A behaviour—the sort of behaviour exhibited by go-getting ambitious clock-watchers. A lack of regular exercise also increases the chances of getting atherosclerosis and therefore of cardiovascular disease.

The prevention of heart disease can only be achieved by

removing the risk of atherosclerosis. This is best done by maintaining an ideal weight, eating a healthy low fat diet, not smoking, keeping alcohol levels within sensible limits, reducing stress levels by relaxation and better management of time, and performing regular exercise.

The Healthy Heart Plan

Check with your doctor that you can follow this plan

- Take stock of your personal situation and assess the current risks to your health that are happening as a consequence of your lifestyle.

- Find out if you exhibit Type A behaviour by answering the questions in Table 4 (see pages 54 and 55).

- Decide to alter those areas of your life which are posing unnecessary risks to your cardiovascular system.

- Ensure that your weight is within the ideal range. Determine to lose weight if you are obese.

- Adopt a healthy balanced diet. Choose meals in hotels and at business lunches with care.

- Control your drinking habits. Do not drink regularly. Soft drinks should be drunk more frequently. Use mixers in spirits.

- Give up smoking. Declare no-smoking areas in the office. Use hotels which offer no-smoking bedrooms and no-smoking public rooms.

- Take regular exercise. Three 20 minute walks each week may be all that is needed. Do not embark upon an exercise programme without medical advice.

- Reduce the stress in your life. Learn to manage time effectively. Adopt the Healthy Mind Plan of Chapter 1.

- Assess your behaviour patterns. Attempt to control Type A tendencies. If you cannot do this on your own, then seek help from professional therapists.

- Get your blood pressure checked on a regular basis. Any increases may need treatment by a doctor to help reduce the risks of heart disease and strokes.

3
A Healthy Body

Whilst the previous chapters have emphasized the importance of a relaxed frame of mind to help reduce stress, and preventative action to lessen the chances of heart and circulatory disease, neither of these two valuable ideals is of much help unless we look after the body as a whole. It would be pointless reducing the stresses in life, and avoiding heart disease, if we laid ourselves open to other serious conditions. It is therefore vital that all executives interested in improving their health generally, look after the whole body, and not just the mind and the heart, although these two positive steps will have a dramatic effect on a person's life expectancy. Executive life can be at the root of more serious conditions, though, which can be just as harmful to any individual as heart disease, or stress. Consequently, this chapter outlines a whole host of different areas of ill-health to which executives may fall prey, and offers advice on how to combat them.

Cancer

After diseases of the heart and of the circulatory system, cancer is the biggest killer. Cancer is a generic term which actually refers to a wide variety of conditions, but all cancers taken together account for one death in every five. So, although the problem of cancer affects fewer people than heart and circulatory disease, it is nevertheless a major problem. In England and Wales alone 150,000 people are dying of cancer each year. One woman dies of breast cancer every 50 minutes in the United Kingdom. In the United States 50 people die of cancer every hour of every single day and night.

Unlike many cases of heart disease, which produce sudden, frequently unexpected deaths, cancer is generally a slow killer. Sufferers of cancer are often forewarned of their impending death, making cancer one of the most feared illnesses of all. The word cancer itself is full of terror. Many people are even afraid to say it out loud, only daring to mention it in a half whisper, in case the mere enunciation of the word could lead to the disease taking a hold.

However, there are many different types of cancers and they have many different causes. The 100 or more different cancers known to doctors are due to a variety of causes, including toxic chemicals or radiation, but generally there is no known specific cause for many of the cancers which afflict humans. Although medical research into the causes of cancer continues all the time, doctors are often more concerned with treating the condition and improving a sufferer's life expectancy, and the quality of life, than trying to determine causes. However, despite the fact that so few causes of cancer have been isolated, some very strong associations have been highlighted which should not be ignored. One of these is the link between cancer and smoking.

Smoking and cancer

As explained in the previous chapter, the biggest threat smoking poses to a person's health is in its ability to increase the chances of heart and circulatory disease. The second biggest threat to health from smoking is its gripping link to cancer. In the United Kingdom the biggest type of cancer is that which affects the lungs and their associated tubes. Lung cancer is responsible for more than one cancer death in every five.

The simple fact about these deaths is that the vast majority of the people who succumb to lung cancer also smoke. As women have begun to smoke more and more, so their likelihood of falling victim to lung cancer has risen, so much so that it now kills more women than breast cancer.

Since the report from the Royal College of Physicians of England was published in 1962, there has been growing evidence to support the notion contained in the RCP's 'Smoking and Health' that smoking actually causes lung cancer. No one really knows exactly how, but the millions of smokers who have died as a result of lung cancer bear witness to the fact. Smoking has also been linked by doctors to cancers of the larynx (voice box), the mouth, the gullet, as well as the pancreas, the bladder and the kidneys. Smoking is a common factor in a whole host of cancer cases. The only method of reducing the chances of cancer due to this cause is not to smoke. Avoiding smoke-laden rooms so that you do not inhale passively the noxious material is also a good idea if you wish to minimize the risks of tobacco.

The fact that cigarette smoking actually causes lung cancer has been confirmed by the United States Department of Health and Human Sciences in its report 'Smoking and Health' published in 1979. That report reveals that the risks of suffering from lung cancer are increased with the number of cigarettes smoked, by starting smoking at a young age, and by using higher tar brands. However, even though the low tar brands seemed to be responsible for fewer instances of lung cancer than high tar types, groups of people who smoked them still had many more cases of cancer than non-smokers. The report also revealed that smoking a pipe or a cigar was associated with a lower incidence of lung cancer than smoking cigarettes, but that this lower level was still greater than that seen in groups of non-smokers. Moreover, pipe and cigar smokers were at the same risk of developing cancer of the larynx as cigarette smokers. They also had the same risk of contracting cancer of the mouth and the gullet. Consequently, choosing to smoke a pipe or a cigar will not cut down the chances of cancer dramatically. Only non-smoking will.

Although no one is exactly sure as to how smoking causes cancer, a major factor is the inhaled material which causes some of the cells of the lung, or the airway tubes, for example, to undergo dramatic genetic changes. As was explained in Chapter 1, all of our cells contain coded instructions which enable them to build up our body and perform the necessary functions. Inhaled smoke seems to trigger off changes in the genetic instructions in certain cells, making them undergo rapid, uncontrolled growth, resulting in the overproduction of uncontrollable cells—a 'growth' or a 'tumour'. In a word, cancer.

For some unknown reason some cells are particularly prone to attack from such stimulants as smoke and they can be triggered off into producing cancers. This is probably due to the individual susceptibility to disease mentioned in Chapter 1, and may explain why there are a few people who seem to be able to smoke and apparently not suffer from cancer. This element of individual susceptibility is the reason why some people who smoke get heart attacks, whilst others get lung cancer, and some escape such illnesses altogether, though they are few and far between. At the moment, there is no way of predicting whether or not a smoker will be particularly susceptible to either heart disease or lung cancer, and so the only way around the problem is to take steps to avoid both of these conditions caused by smoking. Basically, give up the deadly habit.

This may be easier said than done, especially for executives. Business men and women who smoke may well do so to help relieve the pressures of the day. Cigarettes may well provide some executives with an 'escape valve'. Once this release mechanism has been started, it becomes a habit. Tobacco contains an addictive drug, nicotine. Once this takes a hold it is very difficult to give up, and all the statistics in the world will not be able to help many smokers to give up. Nicotine addiction is a serious problem and one which is just as difficult to shake off as any other drug problem.

There are many suggested remedies for nicotine addiction which are supposedly able to help people to give up cigarettes. Some of these remedies can be assigned straight to the quackery dustbin. The first port of call for any executive trying to give up smoking is not the pages of the local newspaper advertising some gimmick, but the office of a sensible and sympathetic family practitioner. Whilst doctors may gently scold an individual for smoking, they realize that it is an addiction and needs careful therapy to effect a successful withdrawal from the drug.

Smoking creates two dependencies: firstly, there is the physical addiction to nicotine; secondly, there is the psychological addiction to cigarettes, cigars or pipes. Only by attacking these two particular problems will any attempt to give up smoking be successful. So the psychological methods of attempting to give up smoking, such as behavioural therapy, or attempts at self-control, fail to take into account the physical addiction of the nicotine. Similarly, drugs which may help control nicotine addiction are not very effective without attention to the psychological dependence upon smoking. In addition, giving up smoking leads to some pretty nasty side-effects known as 'the smoking withdrawal syndrome'. These include headaches, drowsiness, irritability, a lack of ability to concentrate, and stomach upsets.

Without the psychological support necessary to cope with this syndrome, anyone attempting to give up smoking may soon be tempted back into puffing away again, if only to get rid of the side-effects of giving up! Indeed, amongst people who attempt to give up smoking, something like eight out of every ten are smoking again within a year of starting their non-smoking trial.

One method of achieving a higher chance of giving up smoking is the use of a special chewing gum which contains nicotine. Nicotine itself does not cause cancer or heart disease; it is the other components of cigarettes which do this. So a gum which contains nicotine will be relatively harmless. The idea is that under controlled conditions, where psychological and medical support is provided, smokers who want to give up replace the cigarettes with gum. Chewing a piece of this special gum every two to three hours has the same psychological effects as smoking fairly heavily, except that there are no harmful toxic substances to increase the chances of heart disease and cancer. Over a year or so of using this gum people can gradually be weaned off it until their dependence on nicotine has been controlled. Consequently, used correctly in people who are motivated to success, the psychological problems can be dealt with whilst the nicotine addiction is gradually controlled without adding further risks to health. The disadvantage to the gum is its price. In the UK it is not available on the National Health Service, but can only be obtained privately from doctors. However, executives with a reasonable disposable income, as most have, may well find that the cost of the gum is around the same as that of their harmful supply of 'cancer sticks', as many people now call cigarettes.

Acupuncture and hypnosis have also reported some degree of success in helping people to give up smoking. It is wise to check the credentials of people offering 'alternative' therapies. Ask your family doctor to refer you to one he respects, rather than search one out for yourself. Whilst most people offering alternative therapies are well-trained and skilled at their jobs, there is the possibility that some unscrupulous practitioners could charge for services they are unable to deliver effectively. The best way to attempt to give up smoking and so avoid the chances of cancer is to seek help from a family practitioner in the first instance.

Diet and cancer

Even if someone is able to give up smoking altogether, or preferably never start, there is still the risk that cancer may develop. Smoking is more strongly linked to the development of a variety of cancers than virtually any other activity with which we come in contact day to day. However, there is growing evidence and support from doctors for the notion that our diets may contribute to the risk of developing particular kinds of cancer.

There is not much solid evidence in the field of nutrition and cancer, and some wild claims have been made in the past. Indeed, there is hardly a year goes by without some foodstuff being criticized, loud and clear, for its cancer-inducing properties. If we all left out the supposedly harmful foods we would be very hungry indeed! However, there is some evidence which suggests a link between our overall dietary habits and our chances of developing cancer.

People who have a high intake of fats in their diets for instance, tend to suffer more from cancer of the rectum or cancer of the breast. (Men should note that cancer of the breast does not only affect women, males suffer too.) In Japan, for example, where traditionally the diet has been low in fats, the incidence of breast cancer has been much lower than that of other Western nations. However, the incidence of breast cancer is now rising in Japan, and health officials point out that there has also been a similar rise in the eating of what could be loosely called an American or European diet—one which has a much higher content of fats. This does not prove anything, but it does cause doctors at least to suspect that there may be a relationship between dietary fat and, for example, breast cancer.

Too much alcohol is known to be behind some cases of cancer, in particular cancers of the liver. Liver cancer is one which takes a hold rapidly and death usually occurs only months after diagnosis. Practical prevention of liver cancer for executives can best occur by adopting a sensible approach to drinking alcohol.

Low fibre diets have also been linked to cancers of the intestines. No one is quite sure why, but fibre is known to aid the movement of foodstuff through the gastrointestinal tract, and a lack of it may cause irregularities of these movements. People who are obese, which is being only 10 per cent over ideal weight (a women whose ideal weight is 8½ stones (119lbs, 54kg) needs only to be just over 9 stones 5lbs (131lbs, 59.5kg) to be termed obese by doctors) also tend to suffer more frequently from cancers of the intestinal tract. So eating the right amount of food is also a good idea to help prevent cancer.

No one has yet solved the diet and cancer riddle, but doctors who specialize in the care of cancer patients are increasingly favouring a 'healthy diet' as a means of reducing the likelihood of contracting cancer.

This healthy diet is the same sort of diet that heart specialists recommend to avoid heart disease. The cancer-avoidance diet, as some people have called it, consists of a high protein, low fat diet which has plenty of fibre too. Following the dietary tips in Chapter 2 should help reduce the likelihood of cancers, if the theories currently suggested by many cancer specialists are proved correct.

Executives and cancer

Many executives will be at increased risk of certain cancers. One factor affecting this is their age: cancers tend to strike at older people. Prior to the age of 40 cancer is a very rare event indeed. In fact, only 2 or 3 people in every 1,000 under the age of 40 is ever diagnosed as having cancer each year in the UK. By the age of 60 this has gone up threefold to 9 in every 1,000 and by the age of 80 this has again doubled to 18 people in every 1,000. Since the vast majority of executives tend to be middle-aged or older, they will also stand a greater chance of suffering from cancer than the general population. However, preventative measures need to be taken for as many years as possible, rather than just at the time of greatest risk. Therefore, younger executives should not attempt to leave prevention until after their 40th birthday! The earlier preventative efforts begin, the greater their chance of success.

Prevention of cancers is nowhere more necessary than among workers in those industries where specific links to certain cancers have been identified. Executives who work in these sorts of industries should ensure that they take all the necessary precautions. For example, people working in the dye manufacturing industry are more prone to cancer of the bladder, and people who become exposed to radiation, such as those in laboratories which work on radioactive samples, can increase their chances of some blood cancers. The risks can be minimized for workers in these industries and there are government instructions for safety in many instances. Executives should ensure that they too adopt any necessary safety procedures when coming into contact with areas of the building which are designated as high-risk. Not doing so would only be likely to contribute to an increased chance of that executive suffering from cancer, especially if the executive flouts any safety precautions on a regular basis. Civil engineers, for example, wear hard hats for their own obvious safety. Industrial managers too should be sure that they adopt their own industry's safety codes to minimize their risks of being harmed.

Screening and cancer

Apart from taking preventative measures, such as giving up smoking, adopting a healthy diet, and abiding by safety rules, the risks of death due to cancer can further be reduced by careful screening. Cancer is best treated when it is in its early stages and has not had a chance to take a hold and begin its uncontrollable and fatal spread. Since most cancers do not produce symptoms until they are well advanced, the only real way of spotting many cases of cancer is by looking regularly to see if they are present.

Screening the entire population for every cancer on a regular basis would be an enormous task, and one which would be a tremendous financial burden upon the health service. Consequently, most countries restrict their screening to those cancers which have a chance of being successfully treated if caught early enough, or where a cure is possible. One cancer for which screening is supremely efficient is cancer of the cervix, the neck of the womb.

Cervical cancer is the third most common type of cancer in women—lung cancer and breast cancer hold the top two positions. It is most common in the lower socioeconomic groups, but women executives still stand a chance of suffering from the disease if they have any of the risk factors—an early age at which sexual intercourse first began, sexual activity with more than one partner, and vaginal infections. Recent evidence suggests that cervical cancer is due to a virus. There is little hard evidence to suggest that the oral contraceptive Pill causes cervical cancer, as has been claimed in a number of reports. There has been much debate about this, and it seems that the role of the Pill in cervical cancer is the sexual freedom it offers women so that they can have sex with a number of different partners. This, in turn, makes the transmission of a virus much more likely. It has been suggested that the use of condoms may well prevent the transmission of the virus thought to cause cervical cancer. Whatever the reason for the cancer, however, it is one of the few totally curable cancers, *providing* it is detected early on.

Screening for cervical cancer is a simple operation and women at risk of contracting the disease should have a 'smear test' (sometimes called a 'pap smear') every three years, say leading medical authorities. A woman who is at risk is any sexually active woman. There has been much debate about who should be screened for cervical cancer with cost-conscious politicans claiming that those most at risk are women over the age of 35. However, cancer experts are agreed that any woman, regardless of her age, who is sexually active should have regular smear tests to ensure that an early cancer is spotted. These smear tests can detect irregularities in the cells of the cervix which occur *before* a cancer develops. Treatment can then take place to remove the irregular cells and thus avoid the cancer. In China, many commercial organizations have provided smear tests every year or two for their women employees. As a result, the incidence of cervical cancer has dropped by an amazing 97 per cent in the women employees of the companies offering the test. Management in Western nations could take note of this and so reduce the number of deaths from cervical cancer each year.

Another cancer which can be detected early on by a simple screening test is breast cancer. In most cases lumps in the breast are not cancerous, but are usually just fluid-filled cysts which can be easily and quickly removed. Women over the age of 35—the age of many budding executives—are most at risk of developing breast cancer. Such women should examine their breasts every month to look for lumps, and if they find any, they should report them to a doctor who will arrange for them to be investigated.

Examining the breasts is not a difficult operation for women, and can be made a pleasurable experience rather than a monthly chore, by asking a sexual partner to help with the examination. The first step in the simple examination is to stand naked in front of a mirror and look at the breasts. Can you see any change in shape or size since you last checked? Is the skin dimpled or puckered, especially around the nipple? If so, report it to your doctor. Raise your arms above your head and check for changes. Then press your hands on your hips. Then feel each breast for lumps. Lie down and put your left hand under your head. Now feel your left breast with your right hand, using the palm of your hand, not your fingertips. Then, put your right hand under your head and feel your right breast with your left hand. If you feel anything unusual make an appointment with a doctor to check out the problem. If nothing is wrong, then just mark the diary to remind you to check again next month.

Simple screening tests like this are not restricted to women. Men should regularly examine their testicles for signs of cancer. Testicular cancer is the most common form of cancer in men under the age of 35. Like cervical cancer it is potentially totally curable. All that needs to be done to screen for the cancer is to check each month for the presence of hard, painless lumps in each testis. Simply feeling the testicles is all that is required, and like breast screening the clinical nature of the checking can be removed if it is performed with the help of a sexual partner.

Other cancers can also be spotted by the early warning signs shown in Table 6. For example, cancer of the colon is a common cancer and is accompanied by any kind of alteration in bowel habit which is persistent, such as mild diarrhoea. Also, blood on the toilet paper may be a sign of bowel cancer, and should not be dismissed as 'piles'. Bowel cancer is one which spreads only slowly, so treating it early with surgery can be an effective cure.

The effectiveness of treatment for this sort of cancer, providing it is detected early on, only goes to show the enormous efforts that are being made and the success being achieved by the worldwide community of cancer researchers and specialists. A cure for all cancers is a long way off, and the much heralded-treatments of drugs like interferon are only really effective in a small number of extremely rare cancers. Despite this, any executive who is diagnosed as suffering from cancer should not give up hope.

Table 6
EARLY WARNING SIGNS OF CANCER

- Sudden loss of weight without dieting
- Unusual tiredness
- Blood in faeces, or on toilet paper
- Persistent change in bowel habit, either diarrhoea or constipation
- Painless lump in the breast
- Painless lump in the testicle
- Persistent cough, especially if blood is coughed up
- Indigestion
- Blood in the urine

Cancer and the mind

There is growing evidence, and many anecdotal reports, to show that attitude of mind is an important aspect in the effectiveness of cancer treatment. Those people who do not 'give up' and who are prepared to fight their condition seem to benefit more frequently from treatment.

There is also evidence that our minds may well play a role in the development of cancer in the first place. Doctors report that those people who worry that they are suffering from cancer, needlessly, are often the types of people who eventually do succumb to the disorder. There is also evidence from researchers in the United States which shows that those people who suffer stress may well be doing physiological damage to their systems which makes cancer more likely.

Stress appears to alter what is known as our 'immunological system'. This is a complex system of cells and chemicals throughout our body which helps fight off invading infections and so on. The immune system also appears to have a role in protecting us against cancer. Studies in animals have shown that if you subject one group of animals to stress, and another group is allowed to carry on normally, those who have been stressed tend to suffer from cancer. Cancerous cells implanted into their bodies grow, whereas cancer cells implanted into non-stressed animals die shortly after the end of the experiment.

Whilst this is not conclusive evidence, it does suggest that there is a link between stress, our immune system, and our ability to fend off cancer. Too much stress may make us more prone to cancer and this is an additional reason as to why executives, particularly those over 40, should be sure that they live as stress-free a life as possible.

Digestive troubles

Stress is also linked to problems of the digestive system. A common problem for many executives is indigestion. The number of business lunches, cocktail parties, drinks with the boss, and so on, puts a strain on the digestive system; stress on top of this can trigger symptoms of indigestion.

As outlined in Chapter 1, the response to stress orchestrated by the body's hormonal system, is to redistribute the blood supply so that energy and oxygen is provided to the muscles where it is most likely to be needed in the event of having to deal with the stressor or run away from it. Consequently, the large amount of blood which normally services our digestive tract is whisked away leaving our stomachs and intestines in the lurch temporarily. In other words digestion ceases during times of stress. Given this stop-start digestive process in times of stress, it is not surprising that the stomach and intestines complain and produce symptoms of conditions such as indigestion. The precise mechanisms by which stress induces digestive trouble is not understood, but what is known is that people who suffer from stress also frequently complain of indigestion and other digestive upsets.

One reason why stress may lead to indigestion is the fact that when we are under stress we tend to swallow air unconsciously. This air can go into the stomach and will lead to the well-known symptoms of wind. A reduction in stress will cut down on this problem. However, the stereotype of the obese executive puffing away on cigars and drinking yet another brandy as the archetypal indigestion sufferer is in fact not quite true. Whilst this sort of unhealthy individual would seem almost certain to be a prime candidate for indigestion, in actual fact most indigestion sufferers are women. Some 60 per cent of sufferers of indigestion are women in their middle to late years. Generally the trouble begins in the child-bearing years, during pregnancy, when the growing baby pushes on the digestive tract, thus impeding the natural process of digestion.

Another factor in indigestion is smoking. People who smoke tend to suffer more frequently from symptoms of indigestion than non-smokers. According to American research this may well be due to the fact that smoking lowers the levels of chemicals called 'prostaglandins'. These are hormones which have a variety of roles in the body, one of which appears to be to protect the stomach from the acid produced to aid digestion. Too much acid can cause the well-known symptoms of heartburn and indigestion, while the presence of prostaglandins helps avoid these symptoms by protecting the stomach lining from the acid. By smoking and reducing the levels of these prostaglandins people are opening themselves to attack. The rule therefore is to not smoke if you wish to cut down the chances of indigestion.

Smoking is also implicated in a more serious digestive problem which gives rise to symptoms of indigestion—the problem of ulceration. Ulcers of the stomach or of the duodenum—the part of the intestine leading from the stomach—are common problems among executives. Indeed there is the old joke about the boss who claimed 'I don't get ulcers, I give them.' Smoking, however, is much more likely than bosses to help produce an ulcer, because it reduces prostaglandins, diminishing the protection of the stomach from attack by acids, thus leading to the possibility of an ulcer. Ulcers are formed in a complex manner, but increased acid production does appear to be common in the vast majority of cases. By smoking, and reducing the natural protection of the digestive system to the acid, the likelihood of an ulcer forming is increased.

Smoking, though, is not the only factor which influences the formation of ulcers. Stress is common in many cases. As was mentioned earlier, stress is not a factor peculiar to executive life; it is common to all of us. Consequently, ulcers are not necessarily linked to executive life. Indeed, there is evidence to suggest that ulcers of the stomach are more common in the poorer socioeconomic groups. However, that does not mean to say that executives will not be prone to ulcers. A combination of stress, alcohol, too much rich food, and smoking, is likely to lead to the possibility of a painful ulcer. Consequently executives need to be sure that they keep their levels of stress down, adopt sensible drinking habits, eat a sensible diet, and cut out smoking, if they wish to avoid an ulcer. The reduction of stress should not be overlooked since increased stress is associated with higher levels of alcohol intake and more regular smoking. So reducing stress will also avoid excesses in these other risk factors for ulcers too.

Stress reduction will also help in another widespread digestive problem. The 'irritable bowel syndrome', or as it used to be called, 'the spastic colon', is strongly linked to stress. This is a painful condition which, while not pathologically dangerous, is uncomfortable, unsettling and worrying. The worry about what might be wrong only adds further to the stress which is thought to be responsible for a large proportion of cases of irritable bowel.

Irritable bowel is the pain and cramp caused by irregularities in the natural movements of the intestines. The contents of our intestines are moved along by a gentle muscular action known as peristalsis. Stress, by halting the process of digestion, can interrupt this natural muscular action, causing the peristaltic movement to become irregular and resulting in pain. The best prevention is to avoid stress, although particular foods may also cause trouble in certain individuals and these should be avoided too.

Occasionally, the symptoms of irritable bowel may mimic those of cancer of the intestines, so it is always wise to check this sort of problem with a family practitioner, rather than attempt any self-treatment. However, taking action to avoid stress as laid out in the Healthy Mind Plan (see pages 45 and 46) will probably be extremely helpful to many sufferers of irritable bowel.

Irritable bowel is also linked to irregular mealtimes. Often executives may rush out of the house in the morning, skipping breakfast, then find they have too little time for a proper balanced lunch, and then go into a heavy three-course dinner at some function in the evening. This puts a strain on the digestive system and may cause all sorts of troubles, particularly irritable bowel and indigestion. Time management and careful planning is an important means of avoiding the rush in the morning and missing out lunch. This erratic pattern of eating also leads executives to consume numerous snacks during the day in an attempt to get a much-needed boost of energy. This is just the sort of eating pattern that leads to another problem which is a 'disease' of middle-aged executives—obesity.

Obesity

People are defined as obese if they are 10 per cent or more above their ideal weight range. Ideal weight depends upon height and sex as shown in Table 5 (see pages 59 and 60). In most cases, the extra fat which makes people obese is gained simply as a result of eating much more food than the body requires. Whilst munching snacks and energy-providing chocolate bars may not appear to be a means of overprovision, in actual fact it may well be one of the main reasons behind the weight gain of busy executives.

Some chocolate bars can contain as many as 500 kilocalories—a fifth of the day's requirements of a desk-based man. If that is washed down with a couple of pints of lager at lunchtime, then the kilocalorie intake will have shot up to around 1,000 kilocalories—almost half the day's requirement, and roughly the entire needs of someone trying to diet! If such a busy executive then goes out to dinner at a function that evening, has a couple of gin and tonics to begin with, half a bottle of wine with the meal, and three courses of food, then the day's intake could well have soared to around 3,000 kilocalories—almost half as much more as would be necessary for the body's requirements. Each extra 1,000 kilocalories over and above the daily requirement will be stored as fat. If this extra level of eating is maintained for around three days 1lb (0.45kg) of extra fat will be formed. Eating only 500 kilocalories extra—the kilocalorie value of some chocolate bars—each day, will put on 1 stone (14lb, 31kg) in three months. A 10 stone person can become obese in three months, simply by eating slightly more than he or she requires. Obesity is not something which requires huge excesses.

An executive who finds that there is not enough time for breakfast, or who thinks that a couple of quick pints will do at lunchtime, is just the sort of person at risk of obesity. What is needed is an attempt to manage time better so that there are enough minutes in the day to eat proper filling, wholesome, balanced meals. Three meals a day will not make people fat if the meals are well balanced and provide only the daily kilocalorie requirement. So a breakfast of orange juice, cereals with skimmed milk, together with black coffee and a slice of wholemeal toast spread with a low calorie margarine, will only provide around 240 kilocalories. If a lunch of fish with fresh vegetables is eaten and mineral water drunk,'the day's total will still only reach around 800 kilocalories, leaving enough space in the day's requirements for a meal at an evening function. The lack of lunchtime alcohol reduces the total kilocalorie intake, helps afternoon work performance, and reduces the risk of heart and liver disease. Indeed some firms, notably American multinationals, ban lunchtime alcohol.

This simple example illustrates that it is possible to eat plenty of food, yet still only consume the daily energy requirements. Naturally, some days will be excessive, say at a conference or at a sales meeting where a large breakfast is followed by a three-course lunch and then a cocktail party and formal dinner in the evening. However, these occasional indiscretions are allowable. It is the overall kilocalorie intake which is important. No one is suggesting that executives should withdraw from the business practice of lunches, or of dinners, or of entertaining in general. What executives should do though, to reduce the risks of becoming obese, is plan their time more effectively so that a breakfast is eaten—this will fill the stomach making it less likely that the secretary will be dispatched for another chocolate bar mid-morning! Regular unhurried lunches will also be possible with effective time management. Lunches are vital if executives are not to demand yet more snacks in the afternoon. Our bodies have what is known as 'a post-prandial dip' during the afternoon. Basically this means that the energy reserves in our blood supply drop to a low point during the afternoon, which is why we frequently feel tired and less able to concentrate at this time. Executives who skip lunch may find that a chocolate bar, or some other snack gives a much-needed boost to failing energy. However, the need for this 'fix' can be avoided by a balanced lunch, which will not only prevent a sudden drop in energy supplies, but will also be likely to have fewer fat-inducing kilocalories than the packet of crisps and a couple of bars of chocolate at three o'clock!

If you are already overweight, then you will need to diet in order to lose those extra pounds. Whilst there are some medically approved diets which will help you lose weight extremely rapidly, these are probably best reserved for those people in whom the excess weight is a severe and imminent threat to life, or for some other reason why large amounts of fat need to be shifted quickly. These diets are made up mostly of nutritious liquids which provide only a small number of kilocalories. For most executives, using one of these rapid weight loss diets for a few weeks would be impossible. Conducting business as normal would be rather difficult for many executives if they could only drink a variety of liquids—the business lunch would disappear almost certainly! For most executives, the simplest and time-honoured method of losing those extra pounds is just to eat less energy than the body requires. If your body needs 2,500 kilocalories a day adjust your diet so that you consume around 1,500. In three days you will lose 1lb (0.45kg). There are no magic cures for obesity. Losing weight is a slow process. This is necessary since you need to re-educate your stomach at the same time so that you will not put on weight again once the diet is over. If you eat 1,000 kilocalories a day less than you require it should take around two months to lose 1 stone (14lbs, 6.4kg). Executives can do this without major and radical changes to either their home life or their business life.

Firstly, you should buy yourself a cheap kilocalorie counter and study it so that you get a good idea of the energy contained in the sorts of foods you eat. Then whenever in a restaurant, a hotel, or at home, choose those foods which contain fewer kilocalories, such as chicken (minus the skin), fish (which is grilled, or poached), and fresh vegetables and fruit. It probably comes as no surprise that the foodstuffs which tend to have fewer kilocalories are also those recommended by doctors as components of a balanced healthy menu.

Avoiding obesity is a bonus in a number of different ways. Apart from the effect of excess fat on our appearance, and the associated psychological problems that may bring, obesity also leads to an increased risk of heart disease as a result of raised blood pressure, as we have already seen. Research has shown that in many instances blood pressure can be reduced, and, presumably, the attendant heart disease risks, simply by losing weight. Avoiding obesity is better.

Obesity also leads to a generalized reduction in life expectancy. People who are only 10lbs overweight can expect to live four years less than people who maintain an ideal weight. Obesity is also a risk factor in the development of a chronic disease, which can have truly disabling effects—diabetes.

Diabetes

Diabetes is a disorder in which the body is unable to provide an efficient supply of the hormone insulin. Some people are born with diabetes since their bodies are totally unable to manufacture the insulin molecules. The children who suffer from this kind of diabetes are totally dependent upon regular injections of insulin. They learn to inject themselves with the hormone, and providing they do exactly as their medical advisors say, they live a normal, healthy and happy life. Most of us will come into contact with such insulin-dependent diabetics every day, but we may not realize it.

The vast majority of diabetics, though, are not born with the disease, and are not dependent upon daily injections of insulin. Instead, these people have developed the disease, usually in their middle years, say after the age of 40.

This type of diabetes is basically a function of ageing. The organ which manufactures insulin, the pancreas, seems to be less able to provide the regular, ˜equired levels of the hormone as the years take their toll. So as someone ages, their supply of insulin can become lessened. For most of us this is not a problem, we are still able to produce sufficient insulin to deal with the body's needs. Insulin is used in the process whereby glucose is absorbed into the body. Too little insulin will result in an excess of glucose in the blood and insufficient in the body where it is used for energy. Someone who is obese will require a greater energy suply in order to move, breathe, and so on. Consequently they require greater levels of insulin. If they are unable to produce the amount of insulin to help fuel their body, then the symptoms of diabetes will begin.

Large numbers of diabetics over the age of 40 are overweight. Various studies have shown that simply by losing weight these people can be rid of the symptoms of diabetes—the pancreas produces the amount of insulin required by the smaller body's more modest energy needs. For others, however, treatment is required and in some cases insulin may be necessary. Poorly treated, or untreated diabetes can lead to severe complications. For example, in the UK, diabetes is the largest single cause of blindness. It leads to irreparable damage to the blood vessels at the back of the eye which severely restricts oxygen supply and leads to death of the cells in this area, causing blindness. Only by correctly treating diabetes can this complication and others, such as kidney failure and gangrene, be avoided. Executives who are overweight are at increased risk of diabetes, and if they suffer from any of the symptoms of diabetes they should check the problem out with their doctor as soon as possible. The classic symptoms of diabetes are: tiredness, excess thirst, frequent urination, and increased appetite.

In addition to the risks of complications as a result of diabetes, there is also strong evidence which supports the theory that diabetes may increase the risk of heart disease. This may simply be due to the excess weight which many diabetics carry, but doctors have reported a higher than average incidence of heart disease amongst diabetics. So obese people may also be further increasing their already higher than normal heart disease risk as a result of diabetes.

It is therefore best to try and avoid both by maintaining an ideal weight. Executives should keep an eye on their waistline and try to maintain a balance in their diet. Exercise too will help burn off those extra kilocalories!

Back pain

Exercise is also an important part of the medical community's programme for avoiding muscular or skeletal problems such as back pain. Back pain is a very common problem indeed, and people in desk jobs, such as executives, appear to be particularly prone to this condition. According to the Office of Health Economics in London, a research organization financed by the drug industry, back problems cost British Industry some £1,000 million in lost production as a result of time off work each year.

The Consumer's Association published the results of a survey in the February 1986 issue of the magazine *Which?* and revealed that one in three people had suffered back pain within the previous twelve months, and that one in every two people questioned had suffered back pain at some time or another. One person in every twenty had even had to give up work or change jobs because of back pain. Back pain is therefore a serious and very common problem.

The causes of back pain are extremely varied. It may be a simple muscular problem, or it may be something wrong with the skeletal structure of the spine. In any event there is usually no cure and a doctor's only available treatment is some means of alleviating the pain. Many instances of back pain recover within about three months with no further trouble. Sadly, though, many do not and large numbers of cases remain something of a medical mystery, save the common features which existed in the lives of many sufferers prior to the pain beginning.

Back pain is common amongst people who do not take regular exercise, who have sedentary lifestyles, who are overweight, and who are careless about lifting weights. All of these are factors common to many executives. The all-day sitting of executives is of litle help in maintaining a healthy back, especially if the executive is overweight, and does not exercise.

Preventing back pain is fairly easy, though some measures do call for industry to be more aware of the problem and to provide some items of furniture which will help alleviate it. You would have thought that the economic consequences of back pain would have jolted business bosses into action, but sadly millions of office workers take days off as a result of back pain induced by poor seating and so on (more of this in the next chapter).

The first step in preventing back pain is regular exercise. Swimming is ideal, say doctors, but so too are walking, yoga, and so on—the sort of exercises which doctors promote as reducing the risks of heart disease. The exercise need be done for only about an hour or so each week, and vigorous exercise schedules should be avoided, unless performed under careful medical supervision, since they can themselves induce back problems as a result of straining muscles.

Keeping weight down is another important way of reducing the risk of back trouble. A spine which has to support a body which is 2 stones (28lbs, 13kg) above its ideal weight is going to be put under unnecessary strain and may well be stretched beyond its limits causing 'slipped discs'. Discs are basically shock absorbers which are placed between each individual vertebra of the spinal column. They help stop the bones of the spine damaging each other, as well as preventing the bones pressing on the nerves. When a disc 'slips' it does not, in actual fact, fall out. Rather the centre portion of the disc prolapses into the centre of the spinal column pushing against nerves and against the spinal cord itself. This can lead to intense pain, and frequently leads to severe back pain which travels down the back of a leg.

Posture, bad furniture, and so on are also contributory factors which can lead to back pain. People are advised by back specialists to stand up straight when they walk, and to choose chairs which put their bodies at the right height for their desks and support their backs effectively. Such chairs are particularly important for women office workers who may be pregnant, since almost one in three cases of female back pain arise during pregnancy.

Executives should also not get too involved in moving files around or shifting desks, as they might be tempted to do in the guise of increasing office efficiency. Leave all those sorts of tasks to people who know exactly how to lift heavy objects. There is a skill involved which prevents too much strain on the back. Almost half of all back problems are caused by people lifting or moving heavy objects without any regard to their spines. Another sizeable proportion are sporting injuries. Executives endeavouring to climb the company squash ladder will not only risk a heart attack if they have any risk factors for this, such as smoking, but are also likely to 'put their back out' by overzealous attempts to win matches. The company executive seeking increased levels of fitness would do better to swim three times a week—the risks of heart disease would be reduced and the likelihood of back damage as a result of exercise would be minimized.

Whilst pain in the lower back is the most common, something like three-quarters of all cases, pain in the upper back, around the region of the shoulder and base of the neck is a particular problem for people with desk-bound jobs. Executives poring over papers or books all day long may well find that their necks ache, or that their shoulders hurt.

This problem may be due to fibrositis, a muscular inflammation which generally clears up within a few days or so after the onset of the pain. Fibrositis is a common problem for office workers, and like so many other health problems, is more likely in those people who are suffering from stress. No one really knows what causes this problem, but constant bending over paperwork or a typewriter, for example, may strain the muscles slightly and lead to inflammation. To avoid this problem regular periods of rest between items of desk work are essential to allow the muscles to relax a bit. Try to take a short break between specific items of work—take a walk up and down the stairs for example. The exercise will help your heart, your back, and your mind, and will relieve the tension in your neck muscles.

Psychologists recommend that no one should work for more than 50 minutes every hour. They believe that our concentration and our ability to make decisions is best maintained if we take a 10 minute rest every hour. Such advice not only increases business efficiency, but also helps reduce the likelihood of neck and shoulder pain caused by too long at a desk. Pain and stiffness like that seen in people suffering from the temporary discomfort of fibrositis is also associated with another, more painful and chronic condition, arthritis.

Rheumatoid arthritis

Rheumatoid arthritis is the form of arthritis which is most likely to afflict executives. The other main kind of arthritis, osteoarthritis, is a function of ageing and is rarely seen before the age of 50. Rheumatoid arthritis, however, has its peak incidence between the ages of 35 and 45.

It leads to pain and tenderness in the joints and stiffness in the affected areas. It usually affects the hands or feet to begin with, but spreads to include other joints, such as the knees, elbows and shoulders. The cause of this type of arthritis is unknown, and attacks of pain and stiffness may come and go over the years. Massage and painkillers can help alleviate the problem, but there is no real preventative measure—except to reduce one of the major risks, stress. People who suffer stress seem to be more prone to rheumatoid arthritis. So the stress reduction package offered in the Healthy Mind Plan may well contribute in a small way to a reduction in the risk of rheumatoid arthritis. Reducing stress may also be an important way of avoiding another risk of advancing years, liver disease.

Liver disease

Diseases of the liver are becoming increasingly common in the Western world. It is no coincidence that the amount of alcohol consumed is also generally rising in those countries where the incidence of liver disease is increasing. Alcohol is a major cause of liver disease, and is frequently behind the deaths due to cirrhosis—the most crippling of all of the liver diseases.

Alcohol damages the cells of the liver, amongst other organs, even in very tiny amounts. Just one gin and tonic may start to harm the liver. Fortunately, the liver has an amazing capability of regeneration. Cells which are damaged can be fairly easily replaced, thus helping to reduce the effects of the harm of agents such as alcohol. However, if the alcohol is drunk to excess, the damage can occur faster than the liver can repair it, resulting in a progressive killing-off of the liver.

This continual damage gives rise to a variety of diseases, all of which may proceed to the serious state of cirrhosis unless something is done. Unlike organs such as the kidney, the liver is unable to make up for the damage by getting its sister organ to help with the work. There is only one liver, it has no back-up. Consequently any damage is serious, and potentially fatal. In addition, the liver is the powerhouse of the body, providing mechanisms for the production of energy and for dealing with toxic substances. Any damage can inhibit these processes, thus incurring a greater strain on other systems of the body and provoking the possibility of other complications.

Alcohol is behind a significant amount of liver disease. In the UK, for example, almost 1,000 people die each year directly as a result of drink-related liver disease. It has been estimated that 750,000 people in the UK are at risk of serious disease due to alcohol, and the cost of drink to industry amounts to 14 million days lost production each year at a financial cost of £1,400 million.

Almost everybody drinks; alcohol is a social drug with widespread acceptance. In the UK some £16,000 million is spent on alcoholic drinks alone. Enough beer is drunk each year for every single UK inhabitant to swallow 3½ pints each week. On top of that each individual would have to drink half a pint of wine and cider each week, as well as one measure of spirits in order to have their quota of the total UK consumption. It doesn't sound too much, does it? But when you take into account the fact that almost half the population is too young to drink and 10 per cent of the remainder do not drink, then the figures seem a bit more staggering. Every single person who now drinks would have to swallow some 7¾ pints of beer a week, just over a pint of wine and cider, and two and a half measures of spirits to drink the national amount bought each year. Altogether adults who drink would need to consume 450 pints of alcoholic drink every year in order to swallow the staggering national consumption of 12,576,256,000 pints (7,145,600,000 litres)!

According to medical authorities, the 'safe' level would be around 300 pints of beer a year, less than 6 pints a week. And this level is really only safe if drinking is not a regular event. Consequently, these figures reveal that the British nation drinks far more than is good for its health. On average we drink 50 per cent more than we should. It is therefore not surprising to discover that there are many people suffering from alcohol-related disease, especially of the liver which is the prime target for attack by alcohol.

The role of stress in liver disease, as was suggested earlier, is in the fact that many executives pushed at work—pressurized by boards and bosses to work harder, produce better results, achieve unattainable targets and so on—find solace in a half-bottle of whisky and find that this provides just the right prescription for helping to get rid of the day's problems. Sadly, whilst the alcohol has the short-term effect of aiding relaxation, it also brings the long-term problem of liver disease.

People vary in their response to alcohol largely as a result of individual genetic make-up, as mentioned in Chapter 1. Consequently, there are people who can drink gallons of alcohol and suffer no ill-effects, whereas others may even develop cirrhosis after just a short period of drinking. Generally, though, serious diseases are unlikely to occur unless there has been a long period of regular drinking. Cirrhosis is most likely to develop in people who have been drinking regularly for five years or more. The amount of alcohol consumed does not have to be great—3 pints of beer a day, every day, can lead to cirrhosis within a few years. More likely than cirrhosis, though, is acute alcoholic hepatitis. This is severe damage to the liver, which unlike cirrhosis, is repairable. Cirrhosis is progressive and, unless total abstinence from alcohol is achieved, causes irreversible liver damage. It is possible to recover from alcoholic hepatitis, provided no alcohol is consumed for about four months. Anyone with this disease should never return to alcoholic drinks without a doctor's permission, otherwise cirrhosis is likely.

As stress at work, or from home, may lead to excess alcohol consumption which may be at the root of liver disease, the stress reduction package outlined in the Healthy Mind Plan is a vital means of avoiding the potential damage of alcohol. Any executive who drinks should be sure to maintain an adequate diet. People who drink a lot also tend to skip meals.

As suggested earlier, the tendency to miss meals can result in obesity, with its attendant health risks. But skipping meals also reduces the supply of essential nutrients such as vitamins and minerals. There is some evidence, and anecdotal tales as well, to support the theory that the damaging effects of alcohol are somewhat reduced if a balanced and nutritious diet is maintained. Any executive who drinks should ensure that a good balanced diet is eaten. Then having achieved that simple step forward, attempts should be made to reduce alcohol intake.

As mentioned in the previous chapter on heart disease, there is a growing feeling amongst psychologists and

medical specialists that the key to achieving a reduction in
the risks of alcohol consumption is 'controlled drinking'.
As with trying to kick the smoking habit, attempting to
deal with alcohol abuse requires will-power and careful
attention to both the physical and emotional aspects of the
constant need for drink. People who give up drinking
completely often return to drinking, but people who are
taught to control their drinking habits tend to fare better,
by achieving and maintaining sensible levels of alcohol
intake.

Controlling drinking requires executives to take an
honest and careful analysis of their current drinking state.
For a week or two write down a list of what you drank,
when you drank it, where you drank it, who you were
with, how long you were drinking for, and how much the
drink affected you. Once you have a two-week diary of
your drinking habits, take a long calm look at it. Add up
the number of drinks, total the number of times you drank
alone, and add up the number of hours of drinking. If the
results showed that you drank alone for more than the
short periods of time you were waiting for a client or
colleague, or that if you were drinking every day, then be
prepared for a shock. Such drinking habits are precisely
the sorts of occurrences exhibited by alcoholics and near
alcoholics.

Did you drink more than around 10 pints of beer, or 20
measures of spirits in each week? If so you are in danger.
Did you drink more at the end of a stressful day? Again if
this is the case, then you should ring the warning bells
loud and clear. Such drinking behaviour is going to
increase your dependence upon alcohol, and therefore
further increase the damage done to the liver and the
possibility of cirrhosis.

Having assessed your drinking habits you should then
start to make an immediate attempt to control them. The
management of time will enable you to reduce stresses
and make the 'end of day' relaxing drink seem less
necessary. Set yourself limits and stick to them. Have days
where you do not drink at all. Always choose drinks that
require time to be drunk—add mixers to spirits to make

them take longer. Drink a soft drink at the beginning of any occasion where alcohol is being drunk—it will help fill your stomach and make you drink less alcohol. Drive to the office and to business functions, rather than use public transport. This should ensure, if you are sensible and caring for your fellow road users, that you do not drink at all. In any event, see your doctor. A family practitioner will be able to do some simple blood tests to indicate the extent of any liver damage, and the doctor will also be able to provide the psychological support necessary if you are to be weaned off alcohol. By seeing a doctor any executive will be able to reduce the risks of alcohol to the liver. Female executives should note that although more men suffer from alcohol-induced liver disease than women, this is probably due to the fact that more men drink greater amounts of alcohol. However women are actually more prone to the harmful effects of alcohol—it takes less alcohol in a women to cause damage—and therefore they need to be extra vigilant.

There is another aspect of alcohol abuse to which all bosses should address themselves, and that is the role of the company in providing the means to help people with potential problems, and in creating a working environment where alcohol becomes less of a focal point in many business activities. The British charity, Alcohol Concern, has been promoting its 'Workplace Advisory Service' in a bid to bring home the dangers of alcohol to companies and to individuals. The charity has encouraged a number of firms to adopt an 'alcohol policy' which is a statement of aims to reduce the alcohol problems of employees, and practical steps for achieving this. Innovations such as this seem certain to help reduce the level of alcohol-related liver damage in the executive world.

Alcohol, though, is not the only cause of liver damage which may afflict executives. Hepatitis is inflammation of the liver, which although frequently caused by alcohol, is more often caused by a viral infection. One type of infection, known as Hepatitis B, is particularly prevalent in many parts of the world and affects some 200 million people. It is usually spread from mother to baby during birth, but can be spread by contact with infected blood. Hepatitis B can also be spread by sexual contact, and may even be spread by saliva.

Executives who travel abroad to parts of the world where Hepatitis B is commonly found, such as Asia, will risk infection if they engage in sexual intercourse with a carrier, for example. The disease causes a flu like illness, together with tenderness in the upper part of the abdomen and a yellowing of the skin or whites of the eyes—jaundice. There is a risk that this disease can go on to become cirrhosis, so any executive who exhibits symptoms of hepatitis following a trip abroad should seek medical advice.

For the executive who travels, Hepatitis B is just one of the infections he or she should be aware of.

AIDS

AIDS stands for 'Acquired Immune Deficiency Syndrome'. It is a killer disease for which there is no known cure. The virus which is responsible for causing the disease immobilizes the body's immune system, which, as has already been pointed out, is vital in the defence of the body against invading infections, and possibly of warding off cancer. Consequently a sufferer of AIDS is open to all sorts of infections and people afflicted with the condition die of severe infections and of cancer, not of AIDS itself.

Without doubt AIDS is a severe threat to the health of the human species. It has been taking hold for over ten years, yet only in the middle 1980s has anything really been done to attempt to come to grips with the problem. The AIDS virus had infected one person in every 1,500 by the end of 1986 in the UK alone. One person in every three in parts of Africa is carrying the AIDS virus. It is a major scourge and is something which every executive ought to take as a serious threat to health. Why? AIDS is passed on largely by sexual contact. Despite many denials, claims to the contrary, and attempts to cover up embarrassment, executives, both male and female, engage in sexual activity outside the home, and often outside of marriage.

Male executives do have affairs with secretaries, female executives do have sex with colleagues whilst away on conferences, and executives do visit prostitutes whilst abroad at all kinds of meetings. All of these sorts of activities pose a threat. Whilst they may lead to venereal disease such as syphilis or gonorrhoea, these are treatable conditions which can be quickly cured. AIDS is incurable and it kills. Any executive should take preventative action to ensure that they do not become infected with the AIDS virus. By catching the virus executives could pass on the disease to loved ones without actually suffering themselves. The spread of this killer virus needs to be halted.

There is only one effective way to stop this virus in its tracks and that is for every single person to only ever have sex with one parter. This is an impossibility, though. Executives who travel abroad will know that at conferences, for example, there are frequently temptations for sexual pleasure. A group of 'the lads' may want to organize a trip to the local 'red light district', or there may be an unexpected opportunity for an evening with an attractive member of the opposite sex who is also at the conference. In any event, executives are faced with sexual temptation. If they take part in sexual activity, either whilst away at a conference or in an office affair, the risk of contracting AIDS is a real one. Any executive engaging in sexual activity, outside a regular stable relationship, should always use a condom in order to help prevent the possibility of getting AIDS. Condoms also help prevent the spread of venereal disease, plus, obviously, the potentially embarrassing problem of an unwanted pregancy. The risks of unprotected sex are now too great. The sound medical advice of using condoms is something which every executive should remember, especially when abroad and tempted sexually, since there are many parts of the world which have a much higher incidence of AIDS than others. However, despite the warnings, AIDS is not going to be the most common problem encountered by executives abroad on conferences.

Travel problems

Many executives have to suffer the problems of jet-setting; it is not the glamorous world it is made out to be. The stresses of flying do not help for a start, as well as the problems of dealing with different languages, and a variety of time zones. Executive travel is certainly not an activity, as so often portrayed in films and television programmes, of ease, relaxation, and trouble-free bookings in hotels!

The first problem that executives suffer in terms of travel is setting off for the airport. This is frequently where trouble begins. Flying is a stressful experience, and even seasoned flyers will still suffer a few troubles. Going to the airport is usually the time when people get themselves worked up and needlessly worried. 'Will the airplane be on time?', 'What if it crashes?', 'What if the flight is diverted because of bad weather?' and so on. All hypothetical, usually needless, concerns. The world airline industry has an enviable record. Flights are generally on time, often early. Crashes are rare in the extreme. Flight diversions are also very rare indeed. The international airline network seems to go on, 24 hours a day, 365 days a year, with only a very few hiccups. Yet we still all worry. This only adds to our stress levels, making the chances of heart disease, and all of the other stress-related diseases, much greater. Planning and careful management of time can help alleviate the problem, since this will ensure that all of the uncertainties are taken care of—the car will be waiting at the destination, the hotel room is confirmed, the flight is at 3.30pm and not 2.30pm, and so on.

Once at the terminal building, however, many executives try to ward off the strain of flying by heading straight for the bar. Apart from the dangers of alcohol, as mentioned earlier in this chapter, this is precisely the wrong thing to do. Alcohol is a drug which leads to mild dehydration. The controlled atmosphere of an aircraft has less humidity than the air we normally breathe and, combined with the dehydrating effects of alcohol, it leads to headaches and a dry mouth. To avoid this, drink plenty of water, or soft drinks such as fruit juices. This is particularly important on long haul flights where the bar may be open for many hours, and where the sheer boredom of some flights may turn any executive to drink. Self-control, and plenty of soft drinks prior to the flight, will lessen the need for alcohol. You will not feel so thirsty since you will not have taken a drug which induces dehydration, and your stomach will not be calling out for filling either. Eat the food on the flight, too, since this also helps fill the stomach, and makes you less desirous of something like a gin and tonic which may provide a temporary satiation, but will, in the false atmosphere of the aircraft, only aid the process by which a headache can begin.

The air of the aircraft is also the cause of some, occasionally embarrasing, problems. For technical reasons the air inside aircraft is pressurized to the same pressure as exists around 6,000 to 8,000 feet (1,829 to 2,438 metres) above sea level. This means it has less oxygen than air on the ground, and is also at a lower pressure. Because the air in your body, in places such as the ears, and in the intestines, is at normal pressure the differences can lead to expansion. This can cause earache, embarrassing gurglings from the intestines, as well as a general expansion. So always wear loose fitting clothes when flying off somewhere. Take a walk every couple of hours on long haul flights. This will help reduce the possibility of your ankles swelling as a result of the pressure change. Also, do not smoke on aircraft. The reduced oxygen supply will only increase the likelihood of headaches in smokers. The difference in air pressures is also the reason why you should drink still liquids, and not fizzy ones, since the gas contained in these will only increase the air in your system.

Another difficulty with flying, although a rarity, is travel sickness. In general this occurs most frequently on ships, but a small proportion of people do suffer from air sickness. This is basically caused by confused messages reaching the brain. The eyes tell the brain that the body is in one particular position, yet the various receptors which actually detect our physical position, largely in the ears, tell the brain something different. The result is a feeling of sickness. On an aircraft the best way to help alleviate the trouble is to make sure that you eat—an empty stomach will only make the trouble worsen. Attempt also to get some sleep. Naturally, like all these things, thinking about the trouble only makes it worse, so watching the movie, or talking to a friend or colleague, may help to take your mind off the situation.

Travel sickness tablets are available and generally work well enough, say experts in travel medicine. However, always stick to the stated dose and stop taking them if side-effects occur. Happily, though, the vast majority of executives do not suffer from travel sickness. Many, though, do have trouble from jet lag.

Jet lag is the curious phenomenon of a confused body which thinks it ought to be sleeping when it is awake, which thinks it should be eating dinner when it is about to have breakfast, and wakes us up for a meeting during the middle of the night. We all have our own internal clock which is a rhythmical cycle of events in our body which prepares us for lunch and dinner, and makes us ready for sleep, for example. Unfortunately, the 24-hour business world does not operate on the same principles and executives can find themselves flung into meetings during the middle of the afternoon when their stomach is yelling for breakfast!

There is no magic cure for jet lag, but executives should attempt to control it. Trying to stumble through the day feeling decidedly tired is no good for business, and only adds further stress to the body and mind, adding all the attendant risks outlined in earlier chapters. Controlling jet lag actually starts in the office. The trip needs to be planned and the time managed carefully if the disruption of the internal clock is to be minimized. In general you should always arrive at your destination a day earlier than your meeting. This gives you the chance to sleep and acclimatize to the time of the country. It also lets you wind down from the flight. Also if possible arrive at your final destination at your normal bed-time so that you can go straight to your hotel room and sleep. Avoid alcohol at this time, too, since it will only disrupt the sleep you manage, rather than help it. If you must drink, try something which contains milk. Milk has been shown to be successful in stimulating the production of the chemicals in the brain which help relaxation and sleep. Is it any surprise that so many mothers have sworn by their cup of cocoa?

Once you have slept off your jet lag, you will be ready to face the day in your temporary residence with enthusiasm, and a lower level of stress, than if you had stayed up all night drinking in an attempt to get to sleep! That reduction in stress, and the calm produced by the sleep, will be beneficial no doubt in business as well as to overall health. However, there will be a number of other health threats abroad which should be avoided.

In many countries the sun is stronger than in the UK, or than in many parts of the United States. There is also the possibility that there may be tropical diseases in common occurrence. The heat may induce excess sweating. Local water and ice may not be entirely free of diarrhoea-causing bugs. A simple medical kit, as outlined in Table 7, can help alleviate these problems, and can put an executive's mind at ease knowing that something is available if trouble brews. The ideal traveller's medical kit should contain: a drug such as loperamide to stop any attacks of diarrhoea; water sterilization tablets to purify tap water; an insect repellent cream or spray to get rid of unwanted midges and so on; a sting relief cream to cut down the pain on skin that did become attacked by insects; a mild pain killer; a cream to protect against sunburn; pills for the prevention of motion sickness; anti-malaria tablets; salt tablets to prevent salt depletion in very hot countries; sticking plasters and a packet of condoms. With this kit in your pocket you should be covered for most problems that might arise. However, you will not be protected against tropical diseases if you have not received vaccination prior to your trip.

Problems like cholera, typhoid, yellow fever, and polio

are still widespread in many parts of the world. Careful
planning of trips abroad will allow plenty of time to get
vaccinations. Executives who are in jobs which can
involve flying off to various parts of the world at short
notice really should see their company medical service, or
an airline medical service, to arrange a whole battery of
vaccinations which will provide long-term protection. In
general, vaccinations can be obtained from family doctors,
but some require performing at special vaccination
centres.

When abroad do not forget that hotels have doctors
available if you should need help. All of the hotels which
provided information in the compilation of this book had
access to medical cover, but happily reported that it was
only required on an occasional basis, and generally only
for trivial complaints, most usually stomach upsets.

The executive abroad should pack the following items into
a small bag and carry it in hand luggage so that it is
available for an emergency. The contents of the medical kit
should be sufficient for most eventualities.

Table 7
THE TRAVELLING EXECUTIVE'S MEDICAL KIT

- Water sterilization tablets
- Anti-diarrhoea tablets (e.g. loperamide)
- Travel sickness pills
- Insect repellent
- Sting relief cream
- A mild pain killer
- Sun-screen cream
- Salt tablets
- Anti-malaria tablets
- Sticking plasters
- A packet of condoms

Now whilst stomach pain and intestinal cramps may be a feature of travel, abdominal pain is often a regular feature of being a woman. Female executives may well suffer from the final health problem this chapter will consider, in any part of the world, the 'Pre-Menstrual Syndrome' or PMS.

The Pre-Menstrual Syndrome

PMS, or Pre-Menstrual Tension as it used to be called, afflicts three women out of every four. It is a combination of problems, not least of which is the discomfort of a menstrual period itself. PMS also leads to anxiety, irritability, fluid retention, headaches, breast tenderness, dizziness, and depression. It is caused by a temporary alteration in hormone levels which occur naturally as part of the reproductive cycle.

Surveys have revealed that many women suffer in silence, believing that PMS is the price they have to pay for being female. PMS can be a distressing problem, and the anxiety produced by the condition can worsen it further. PMS is not only personally problematic for women, it causes difficulties in their working and home lives because of the depression and irritability. PMS is also believed to be a major cause for occasional uncertificated days off work. However, PMS is a treatable condition. Family doctors have an array of treatments available for PMS, and any woman executive who suffers from this relentless monthly problem should seek medical advice.

There are also some self-help steps women can take to alleviate the problems of PMS. Firstly, attempt to reduce the stresses in your life. Follow Chapter 1's Healthy Mind Plan. Then try to get the men in your life to understand the condition better. Males who do not understand the difficulties of PMS may be unsympathetic and will provoke arguments and periods of tension when women are suffering from PMS. This will only add to the depression, anxiety and irritability associated with the condition. Both husbands and male colleagues should learn to understand the collection of problems and discomforts which make up PMS. Show them this chapter and tell them to be less critical of your irritability and depressions each month.

Sufferers of PMS could also try taking a course of evening primrose oil. This has been shown to be quite effective in the reduction of symptoms of PMS.

Summary

It would be a narrow-minded executive who attempted to have a healthy heart and a healthy mind, but neglected the other systems of the body. Working life puts a strain in a number of our bodily functions, and the stresses of day to day living also inflict further damage. Consequently, executives seeking to improve the healthiness of their body should firstly ensure that they have as stress-free an existence as possible. Following the Healthy Mind Plan will help reduce the chances of a whole host of problems from stomach ulcers to jet lag. Stress reduction may also be an important aspect of avoiding cancer.

After heart and circulatory diseases, cancer is the biggest killer: it is responsible for one death in every four. Some cancers have been linked to particular jobs and executives who may work in these areas should be sure to adopt the necessary safety precautions. However, the biggest threat to health which is likely to induce cancer is smoking. Give up. Choose hotels which offer special no-smoking areas, sit in the no-smoking compartments of trains. Avoid smoky atmospheres of bars and restaurants whenever possible. Screening for cancers will also spot many types early on, such as those of the breast, the testicles, the cervix, and the rectum. Adopt regular self-examination procedures to keep an eye on your personal situation.

Another major difficulty for many executives is the strain on the gastrointestinal system. A battery of business lunches, gala dinners, cocktail parties and so on all take their toll. Indigestion, stomach ulcers, and the irritable bowel syndrome are all possible problems—all of which are made more likely with the presence of stress. Eating a sensible diet, choosing the right foods as outlined in the Healthy Mind Plan, and carefully choosing restaurants and menus will help. So will the reduction of stress.

Liver disease is also another threat to the executive, particularly because alcohol is such an accepted part of the business world. Adopting sensible drinking habits, controlling excesses, and instituting a workplace alcohol policy will all be helpful in the lowering of chances of liver disease.

Various infections may also affect executives—indeed doctors who provided information for this book indicated that colds and 'flu are one of the major causes of days taken off work. However, a more serious infection will kill anyone if caught—AIDS. The Acquired Immune Deficiency Syndrome is a threat to any executive who engages in sexual activity with more than one partner. Only by adopting 'safe sex' practices will this risk be lessened.

Executives who travel may also fall prone to various infections, such as tropical diseases. Careful planning will allow for necessary injections, and a simple medical kit packed into hand luggage should provide for a variety of problems which may crop up abroad. Jet lag and air travel can be effectively coped with, especially if alcohol is avoided.

Executives may also be prone to various muscular complaints, especially back pain, which is the major contributor to days taken off work in the UK. Good posture, good seating, and regular exercise will minimize the chances of back pain. So too will avoiding lifting heavy weights or at least taking care not to strain the back.

Finally, female executives are likely to suffer from a monthly problem called the Pre-Menstrual Syndrome (PMS). This can be effectively treated, and no woman should ignore the benefits of stress reduction, since anxiety is strongly linked to PMS.

The Healthy Body Plan

- Understand the sorts of problems most likely to occur and make a positive decision to deal with them.

- Check with your doctor that you can follow the rest of this plan.

- Cut down the chances of cancer by giving up smoking and avoiding smoky atmospheres. Adopt a sensible diet, low in fat and high in fibre. Perform simple self-examination tests to check for early cancers. Wear protective clothing and adopt safety precautions in industries where such matters are recommended.

- Reduce the likelihood of muscular and skeletal problems by regularly exercising—swimming and walking are ideal. Ensure that chairs are supportive and hold the back upright.

- Avoid digestive troubles by adopting a sensible balanced diet. Lose weight if necessary, especially as this will also cut down the likelihood of diabetes. Reduce stress to cut down the chances of indigestion and ulcers, and the irritable bowel syndrome.

- Control alcohol intake so that liver disease becomes less likely. Do not drink alcohol every day. Seek medical advice if your alcohol intake is at a high level. Cut down on stress if this is a prime reason for your drinking.

- Adopt safe sex practices to avoid AIDS and other sexually transmitted diseases. Always use a condom in any sexual activity which is not with your regular partner.

- Plan flying well in advance if possible to avoid the stresses of travelling. Avoid alcohol in aircraft. Drink plenty of soft drinks and ensure that you gain some exercise by walking around the cabin in long haul flights. Eat the in-flight meals, and if possible try to gain some sleep. Avoid jet lag by flying well in advance of your business meetings and planning your arrival at your destination hotel at your normal bedtime.

- Take a small medical kit on all business trips to deal with any unexpected minor health problems. Remember that all hotels have a doctor who they can contact for help whenever necessary.

- If you are a woman, get treatment for any symptoms of PMS.

4
A Healthy Workplace

There seems little doubt that a great variety of trivial
complaints such as headaches, muscular pains and so on,
are due to environmental factors, and so all executives
hoping to achieve all-round health should not only assist
their mental and physical health in the manner described
so far, they should also pay attention to their surround-
ings. Generally, the changes required to most office
environments are fairly minor and do not involve vast
expense or knocking walls down and so on. However,
certainly some cash is required and many executives may
find themselves having to demand changes in company
policy or for provisions in budgets to help ensure a
healthy workplace for themselves and their colleagues.
Many bosses may not see the point of spending money
without seeing any immediate benefit, though an increasing number of firms are opting for 'ergonomically
designed' offices which help prevent a wide range of
conditions and complaints. Whilst such offices do not
bring about any immediate financial benefit, it is true,
there is no doubt that in the long run they do help cut
down on staff sickness and improve overall efficiency by
making the office a more comfortable place in which to
work. A few simple improvements to most office
environments can dramatically change the likelihood of
the staff developing a number of minor, but nevertheless
troublesome, complaints.

Chairs

Since many executives spend a great deal of their time sitting down, it is important that the chairs used in offices offer a number of health benefits. The main consequence of bad seating is backache. Poorly designed chairs which do not provide support, and which do not allow the back to be held up straight, are contributors to back pain, and may well be a major cause of back trouble in office workers. A quick trip around a number of offices will reveal a whole variety of different chairs in use. There will be simple fold-up seats, half-broken typists chairs, or plush multi-function leather armchairs for the boss. Most offices will reveal a surprising variety of chairs, which indicates no consistent buying policy and so a lack of regard for the prime function of seating—to ensure workers are comfortable at their desks and allow them to get on with their work easily. Yet backache is the single largest cause of days off work in the UK. Some 58 million days a year are taken off work by people with 'musculo-skeletal' problems, many of which are backache. These are the days which are certified by a doctor, so there may be many more days lost to industry as a result of back pain which leads to people taking the odd day off here and there. Musculo-skeletal problems account for almost as many days off work as circulatory diseases, such is the scale of the problem. It would therefore seem economically important to companies, if nothing else, to provide good seating so that the level of back pain may be reduced. But what constitutes good seating?

Whether at work or at home the best chairs are those which are made of solid materials and constructed properly. Indeed, it makes economic nonsense to purchase cheap and cheerful chairs since they are likely to need replacing more frequently than more solid types which are built to last. Apart from this, though, a good office chair needs to be supportive of the body weight and the right height for the desk or table at which it will be used. Chairs should also have adjustable backrests.

Deciding on the right height for the chair is fairly easy. It should allow you to sit on it comfortably so that your knees are at right angles with your thighs parallel to, and your feet flat on, the floor. Your weight in this position should be supported on your buttocks, and not on your thighs. A chair that provides this sitting position will help maintain a straight back, which will reduce the muscular strains imposed by sitting in any other manner. However, the important point about the chair is that it should allow you to sit at the appropriate height, and since we are not all of the same height the ideal office chair should have an adjustable seat position.

The best office chair will also have an adjustable backrest, which provides support for the small of the back. Again, because we are all of differing heights, this needs to be individually adjusted to the appropriate position. The oval-shaped backrests on traditional typing chairs are excellent back supports and deserve wider employment. Sadly, many executives feel that such chairs are 'beneath their status'—and they are the ones that probably end up with backache!

Since very few executives actually sit still for long periods of the day, the office chair really ought to have wheels to allow free and easy movement. A chair without wheels will mean that unnecessary stretching and bending will occur, putting additional strains upon the muscles of the back.

Having bought a chair with wheels, a backrest, and an adjustable seat height, use it! When you have meetings in your office, sit in that chair, when you have meetings in other offices in the same building, take your chair with you, if possible. Alternatively meeting rooms should have chairs reserved for particular individuals, or at least chairs that can be quickly adjusted to suit. In other words, meeting rooms would be best fitted with adjustable chairs similar to typing chairs, rather than the often-seen non-adjustable, hardly movable armchairs.

Other features of chairs may be needed in certain circumstances. Armrests, for example, are available on many good chairs. However, they are only really necessary if the arms are being held out at length for some time, consequently they provide greater comfort for typists, providing, naturally, that the rests are padded. Headrests may also be required if the head is being bent down for some time—the weight of the head will need some support when it returns to the vertical after being bent down for some time. So headrests may be helpful in providing additional comfort, and avoiding neck pain, in certain occupations.

Executives should not forget, also, the health of people who visit the offices. Chairs for guests, in office areas and in reception, should be comfortable, solid and supportive of weight. The very low down 'sofa' style seats seen in many reception areas are probably not a good idea.

Another point to remember is the quality of car seats. Many executives spend long hours driving to and from meetings. It is important that the car seat is fully adjustable and supportive. You should be sitting upright, but relaxed with your elbows and knees only slightly angled. In other words, don't use cars where you have to sit 'doubled-up'.

Desks

Whilst seating is a vital aspect of ensuring that backs are protected, desks too have their impact on health. Desks are not just functional pieces of furniture upon which papers, books and typewriters may be placed. They are the home of our daily work, and so we should be comfortable using them for a number of hours. Desks should provide sufficient working area, they should be at the right height, and they should be well lit.

Working at a desk which is at the wrong height will put a strain on the back. If the desk is too low the back will need bending, and there will be the additional risk of forever bruising your knees by constantly hitting the desktop. If the desk is too high, shoulder ache will develop because of the necessary contortion needed to reach the work. The height of the desk, like the height of the chair seat, should ideally be adjusted to suit

individuals. Sadly very few desks are height adjustable.
The top of the desk is at the correct height if you are able to
work with your forearms at right angles to your upper
arms. In this position the underside of the desktop is only
a few inches from the tops of your thighs. If you are
particularly tall, with your seat adjusted correctly, the
desktop may be too low. If it can be adjusted do so, but if
not backache and neck strain can be avoided by placing
the desk on solid blocks to raise its height. If this needs to
be done, ensure that any means of raising the desk height
cannot be tampered with or easily moved since this will
put the stability of the desk at risk and may cause an
accident.

   If the desk is too high for a short person, then a foot-rest
can be helpful, though this means the height of the chair
will need adjusting to compensate. This raises the person
nearer to the desktop, thus helping in getting the desk at
the right height for the individual.

   Desk height is an important factor in preventing such
complaints as fibrositis and strained muscles. The use of
desk space is also important in this respect. A cluttered
desk which has insufficient space means that necks will be
craned and backs bent to reach the bits and pieces
required to get on with the work. There should be enough
space on a desk for a central clear area where the work of
the moment can be performed. For many individual
executives this means they need two desks; one for all the
necessary items for work in progress—a telephone, pads
of paper and so on, and a second, possibly at right angles
to the first, for all those elements of work which are
required from time to time during the day, but are not in
constant use. This extra desk may contain reference
books, your time management system, a computer
terminal, and so on. Attempting to fit all of these items on
one desk may be efficient in terms of cost-effectiveness in
the short-term, since you need fewer desks, but in the
long-term cluttered desks lead to inefficiency as well as to
an increased chance of muscular strains and other health
problems. Most executives will require two desks, or at
least one desk and an adjacent table.

The position of the desk in relation to the office layout is also an important factor. Having to turn around every time someone enters the room is not good for your neck or back; in an open plan office having your back to a draught is not ideal; working where sunlight will reflect into your eyes will mean that you will crane your neck to avoid the glare; and so on. The placing of desks requires more thought than just finding out how many can be crammed in to the smallest space!

Office space

There are statutory regulations covering the number of people who may work in a particular amount of office space. International building codes allow for 400 cubic feet of space per occupant of an office; for a room 8 feet high that is a floorspace of 10 feet by 5 feet. Many offices are taller than this, thus reducing the minimum floor space required by such building codes of practice. Into this space is crammed a desk, a chair, and perhaps even a filing cabinet. The suggested minimum is not very large. The increasing trend to the 'open plan' style of office, where walls are replaced by screens and where many people work in one large office, may well reduce the amount of floor space required by individuals by centralizing the filing and so on. The idea behind open plan offices is that they improve communications within the workplace, and give bosses a greater degree of control over their staff—workers are in constant view and can be more closely monitored than if they are huddled away in their own private office. However, open planning does have its disadvantages, particularly for health.

Firstly the reduction in personal space can be psychologically upsetting. It is also more likely to remove the possibility of two desks per person. Consequently, neck strain may result because of the need to keep shifting around the desktop. In addition, open plan offices mean that some individuals will have their back to open spaces, making them crane their necks around to speak to colleagues. This will only add further strain to necks, and increase the likelihood of people taking days off because of various aches and pains. Open planning may achieve an increase in communication and control but it could lead to a higher incidence of odd days off as a result of non-specific ailments brought about as a result of the physical environment.

Another problem with open planning is that it does not always follow for the best positioning of desks. In addition to being in places where workers will not need to crane their necks for much of the day, desks need to be positioned where light, heat and ventilation are adequately provided.

Light

The best type of light for work is natural light. This is generally bright, is easy on the eyes, and unlike some other forms of lighting is not associated with health problems such as headaches. In order to help illuminate work, every office should provide some form of natural light. Windows in offices help in a number of respects. They are psychologically important to avoid a feeling of being 'cut-off' from the outside world. In addition, they are economically valuable since the natural light which shines through them reduces the amount of artificial light required, thus cutting down a company's fuel bills.

Illumination is measured in units called 'Lux'. Each Lux represents one lumen per square metre. A lumen is a measure of light intensity, and represents the amount of light passing through a given area every second. So an area which has a higher Lux figure has more lumens reaching it; that is to say the higher the Lux number, the brighter the area. For example, standing outside on a bright sunny day you will be in a level of something like 100,000 Lux. An overcast day may cut this to 30,000 Lux. A well-lit office, however, will have only around 800 Lux and some may be as low as 300 Lux. Offices are, therefore, comparatively dim, and any amount of extra daylight which they receive will be a bonus. This extra light will be helpful in health terms.

Sitting in the half-dark of a badly lit office, peering at papers, will mean that you will have to put a greater strain on the muscles which focus the eye, as well as bend your back so that you are closer to your work. The result is headaches and backaches. The simple cure is to increase the lighting levels.

Many offices, particularly open plan offices, have the bright light of fluorescent fittings. These provide widespread bright illumination at a comparatively low power consumption and are therefore cheap to run. However, fluorescent lights have been suggested as the cause of a number of health problems for people who have to work under them all day. This is because fluorescent lights can flicker more noticeably than ordinary bulbs. All lights flicker due to the alternating current used in mains electricity supplies; generally, however, this is too fast to become noticeable. With a number if fluorescent lights in an office, though, the flickering may well become noticeable, especially if a tube is old. This flickering has been blamed for headaches, as has the humming which can accompany fluorescent lighting. In both instances the problems can be removed by regular, proper, maintenence. Despite this some people still report being annoyed by fluorescent lights.

Fluorescent lights have also been linked to the development of skin rashes, and in one worrying study, to the development of skin cancer, although the slight rise in skin cancers in the UK is more likely to be due to an increase in the number of people regularly holidaying abroad in bright sunlight where ultraviolet rays—which may trigger skin cancer—are common.

If possible, avoid fluorescent light in offices. It may not have serious health risks, but the flickering and the humming can be troublesome to some workers. Also, if a tube fails you generally have to wait for an electrician to call. With ordinary lamps, bulb replacement is simpler because spares can be kept in drawers or cupboards, which is not always possible with the long tubes used in fluorescent lighting, so that if a bulb ceases working then executives have to continue to work in the dark until someone from the maintenance department supplies one. This sort of problem is precisely what triggers stress. So ordinary lighting does have its benefits, even though it is theoretically more expensive to run.

A problem of ordinary lights, however, is the heat they generate. An ordinary light bulb produces considerably more heat than a fluorescent fitting. An office supplied by a large number of ordinary bulbs may become too warm. However, the problem should be minimized with the use of room thermostats, and in the summer when the problem is likely to be greatest anyway, an office which has plenty of natural light sources is likely to need fewer lights switched on, thus reducing any additional heat. In the winter, when more lights are likely to be on, the extra heat they produce will also cut down on the amount of heating required. So any bosses who use the high costs of ordinary lighting as an argument for installing the supposedly cheaper fluorescent kinds can have their false argument quoshed by an explanation of the savings on heating bills that will be forthcoming!

In terms of health there is a positive benefit from using ordinary, non-fluorescent lighting, and this is so that individuals can control precisely the illumination in their working area according to their requirements. This precision control will mean that all of the areas which require bright illumination will get it; annoying reflections, causing backache and neck strain, will also be avoided. Spot lamps can be positioned over filing cabinets, for example, desks will have desk lamps producing a bright, even light for working and so on. Such lighting arrangements mean that light can be focused where it is most needed, avoiding headache and neckache produced as a result of having to bend and strain in poor lighting conditions. In the best offices lighting will have been properly designed by skilled architects and lighting consultants. It sounds expensive, but it will produce a happier, more efficient, working atmosphere and one which is less prone to causing headaches and so on.

Executives who find that the bosses will not spend the comparatively small amounts required on this sort of project can take a number of practical steps to help themselves. Invest in a couple of desk lamps, and a tall 'standard' lamp. Put the desk lamps so that they throw plenty of light over your working area and use the standard lamp to eliminate any shadows they cause. Make sure the cables are hidden, and not in places where they can cause an accident. If fluorescent lights annoy you, then turn them off. Now your work should be comfortably lit so that you will not strain your neck to see amongst the shadows and the likelihood of headaches being caused by poor lighting will have been eliminated. If you use visual display units, or a computer, you will need to take special care with lighting.

Using VDUs

The visual display units of computers are now in widespread use. Once upon a time only secretaries possessed these machines for use in word processing. Now, with the evolution of highly efficient database systems, and with companies performing accounting functions on computers, the VDU is a regular piece of equipment in the executive's office. Indeed, many executives feel that they have not 'made the grade' unless they have a VDU twinkling away on the side of their desk.

There has been much debate about the health risks of using a VDU, although thankfully, most of the claims about the health risks of working with computers have been exaggerated. There are difficulties caused by using VDUs, but these are problems which are not due to the computer display itself. Usually, these are general problems which cause difficulties whether or not the executive uses a VDU. Such things as headaches, eyestrain and so on, as we have already seen, can be caused by a number of factors in the office environment and are not causally associated with the use of VDUs.

The first problem which must be overcome when using VDUs is the provision of adequate lighting. Incorrect lighting of a VDU will cause operators to strain their neck muscles to see the screen, or over-use their eye muscles to focus on the display. In either event the result is generally a headache. People who do use VDUs do get headaches, but the pain is not caused by the screen, rather it is due to poorly controlled lighting. The best position for any computer screen is at right angles to a natural source of light, This will avoid reflections from the screen, thus making it easier to read and so avoiding unnecessary extra work for the muscles which focus the eye. If fluorescent lighting is used, then the VDU should be placed sideways-on between two light fittings, as this also helps reduce unwanted reflections.

Taking care about where a VDU is situated in an office will help reduce eye-strain and consequently help avoid headaches. However, simply adjusting the position of the VDU in the room will not be enough to avoid all the problems associated with their use. The computer terminal should also be at an appropriate height on the desk. This is generally so that the screen is at or just below eye level. If possible, tilt the angle of the screen slightly or stand the terminal on a suitable platform which will raise it to the best height. The special VDU 'workstations' which most office furnishing companies now provide are ideal since they have a movable platform for the VDU. By getting the screen at the right height neckache can be avoided. Positioning the screen correctly also reveals why it is important that the keyboard is a separate and movable part of the computer. VDUs that have an integral keyboard which is not separate from the screen will pose problems—if the screen is positioned at the right height, then the keyboard may be too high. This will cause undue strain on the muscles of the arm and shoulder causing aches and pains and problems such as fibrositis. The answer is to use computers which have a separate keyboard which can be suitably positioned at the right height and distance from the executive—so that the elbows are at right angles, and the forearms parallel to the floor, when using the keyboard.

Taking simple steps like this when installing a VDU or

A HEALTHY WORKPLACE   133

computer will reduce the chances of headaches and neck pain since you will be able to use the machine comfortably. However, there are some points to remember when actually using the machine. Staring at a screen for hours on end can lead to eye-strain. So too would reading a book or company accounts all day; the VDU does not do anything special to cause eye-strain. However, what appears to have happened with the technology revolution is that the novelty of the machinery has led people to sit at their desks and tinker away with the computer for longer periods of time than might have been given to poring over the latest departmental budget if it were on paper. The result is a strain on the muscles which focus the eyes. Like the rest of your body they need, and deserve, a rest. Never sit at your computer for more than 50 minutes in each hour. Take a 10 minute rest to let your eyes recuperate. This will reduce the possibility of headaches due to eye-strain, and will also improve your concentration and ability to make decisions. The value of rest periods is not just in making it easier to use a VDU!

Another point to remember is that using VDUs often requires looking at the screen and at data contained in hard copy at the same time. Repeatedly moving your head from the screen to the desk, or your lap, will unnecessarily strain the muscles of the neck. The simple answer to this difficulty is a copy stand. This should sit at the side of your VDU and should be at the same height and angle as the screen. You will then be able to compare items on the screen with those in your hard copy with only minor movements of the neck, thus reducing the likelihood of shoulder pains and headaches.

One other problem about VDUs which has gained considerable public attention is their supposed link to miscarriages in pregnant women. This is extremely unlikely. The radiation levels which are given off by VDU screens are rigorously tested. Many other items emit radiation too, such as television sets, and even human bodies. However, the amount of radiation given off by a VDU screen is tiny. In fact, if you sat with your face pressed against the screen for a year you would find it difficult to absorb the same amount of radiation that you will absorb by sleeping in the same bed as your partner every night! IBM has many VDUs in current use, and this company is unable to detect any radiation a mere 2 inches from the screen.

However, despite these assurances there have been claims that the radiation levels produced by VDUs may lead to miscarriages and birth defects. There does not appear to be any real evidence to support this notion. What is known, though, is that stress may lead to pregnancy problems, and women who use VDUs may become worried that the machine may be harmful. This stress may contribute to problems, rather than the VDU itself. The proportion of birth defects and miscarriages amongst women who have worked with VDUs, is, however, not higher than the incidence of these problems amongst women who have not worked with VDUs. This supports the widely held view that VDUs pose no real threat to pregnant women. However, female executives who are concerned should see their doctor who will monitor the pregnancy more closely if requested so that the potential stress can be reduced.

Computer screens have also been the suggested cause for sight problems, particularly cataracts. A cataract is a problem which leads to the lens of the eye clouding over, resulting in blindness. The only treatment is the surgical replacement of the faulty lens. However leading medical authorities, such as the American Medical Association, have declared that VDUs do not produce radiation levels sufficient to cause such biological problems. The Dutch Government Medical Agency has even gone so far as to say that the alleged cataract dangers of VDUs should be 'consigned to the realm of fables'.

The real problems of using a VDU relate to other office matters such as the lighting, and the provision of good chairs and desks at the right height. These will affect all office workers, whether or not they use a VDU. Another environmental problem which can cause health difficulties for all is noise.

Noise

Unwanted noise is one of the problems most likely to
upset any one of us. Human beings tend to become highly
stressed if there is too much noise, especially if that noise
is confusing and loud. We get distracted from our work
because of noise, and excessive noise can lead to
headaches or even migraines. Noise is seemingly endemic
in offices. There are typewriters clacking away, computers
buzzing, people chatting, photocopiers whirring, tele-
phones ringing, and bosses shouting. The average office is
full of noise, and whilst this is unlikely to make anyone
deaf, it is annoying and can therefore lead to stress.
Attempting to diminish or avoid noise in offices is
therefore an important aspect of any attempt to reduce
stress, as well as an efficient means of preventing
headaches.

Sound is measured in units called decibels (dB). Zero dB
is the level of sound which can only just be heard by the
human ear. As the sounds become louder the dB number
goes up. However decibel measurement is on a logarithmic scale; that is to say, for example, that something like
20dB is not twice as loud as 10dB, but is in fact ten times as
loud. A sound level of 40dB would be 1,000 times as loud
as 10dB. Because the measurement scale is logarithmic the
intensity of sound increases tenfold for every ten points
on the scale. The noise levels in the average home may be
around 40dB. These noises come from central heating
systems, passing traffic, children chattering and so on.
The average office will produce noise levels of around
50dB to 60dB—up to one hundred times noisier than most
homes! Consequently lessening office noise seems to be
an admirable goal, if only to reduce the amount of
conflicting sounds so that people may work more
efficiently.

One certain way of increasing general noise levels is to
have an open plan office. This multiplies the number of
people speaking, the number of telephones, the number
of typewriters being used, and so on. This leads to an
increase in noise making it more difficult to concentrate,

harder to hold telephone conversations, and more likely to induce stress and headaches. Bosses may think that open plan offices improve communications, and on the surface they might. But the increased noise levels make for a reduced level of efficiency and can actually decrease the levels of communication by making it much harder for people to listen to important conversations or talk on the telephone.

Reducing the noise levels is possible. Screens can be put up between desks and in strategic corners where noise seems to congregate. Fluorescent lights should be checked so that the hum is reduced. Get the maintenance men to overhaul the ventilation system, too, so that it does not vibrate. Get 'acoustic hoods' for computer printers, and buy the special sound-reduction pads which are available for many typewriters. Noisy streets can be cut off by the installation of secondary or double glazing. It is also possible to buy sophisticated machines which generate noises to mask out the cluttered collection of office sounds. However, a keen eye to office design combined with a few simple common sense steps, such as those outlined above, will probably reduce the need for the installation of such noise-reduction systems.

Atmosphere

Many offices have efficient air conditioning, but many do not. Such offices can become uncomfortably hot during summer months, and incredibly stuffy during the winter. This can lead to alterations in the atmosphere which can be at the root of a number of common ailments reported by executives and other office workers.

The molecules of air around us are constantly moving and vibrating. This movement is rapid and it causes alterations in the structure of the molecules. The molecules either become negatively charged as a result of picking up an extra electron, or positively charged due to the fact that they have lost an electron. Any molecule which becomes charged electrically in this way is called an 'ion'. Ions have been linked with a variety of problems, and the scientific literature contains a number of references to the fact that an excess of positive ions is associated with depression, headaches, lack of concentration and irritability. An excess of negatively charged ions, however, is linked to a happy frame of mind, good concentration and fewer headaches. Sadly, many offices have an excess of positive ions, thus leading to headaches, irritability, and so on amongst workers.

Positive ions may be produced as a result of some kinds of heating or ventilation systems. They are produced by some computers. Hot stuffy atmospheres tend also to have an excess of positive ions in them. All of this means that the average office produces the wrong kind of atmosphere to allow for the smooth operation of work, with low levels of irritability and a lack of headaches amongst staff. Fortunately, the situation is reversible. Machines which 'manufacture' negative ions are available and will pump out ions into the office air quietly and efficiently. They are not expensive; they can cost less than £50 ($75). By using one of these machines to pump out the negative ions into the office, executives can lessen their chances of headaches and so on.

Another atmospheric problem is smoke. There is one clear rule: ban smoking from your own office, and if you have the power, ban smoking from all other offices in your company too. The World Health Organization has declared that people who inhale smoke passively—such as non-smokers in offices where a smoker is puffing away on a cigarette—do stand a chance of getting lung cancer. For this reason alone smoking ought to be banned in all public places, such as offices. If colleagues must smoke, let them do so in their own office. Indeed, they have a legal duty to do so in the UK. The Health and Safety at Work Act says that every worker should: 'take reasonable care for the health and safety of himself and of other persons who may be affected by his acts and omissions at work'. 'Taking reasonable care' is obviously open to interpretation, but in view of the WHO's position on passive smoking, reasonable care could be taken to mean that smokers should not inflict their habit upon others since it could be damaging their health, even killing them. Since smokers are now in a minority, it would not be difficult for executives to gain support to promote and effect a ban on office smoking. However, no such ban is likely to work unless the company provides the necessary psychological and physical support for smokers so that they might be helped to give up smoking.

To ban smoking without making any provision for the smokers would almost certainly lead to their feeling isolated, thus increasing their own stress levels, probably making them smoke more! Consequently the anti-smoking brigade who brought about the ban could also be interpreted as breaking the general provision of the Health and Safety at Work Act quoted above.

Other office hazards

In addition to all the problems mentioned thus far, there are a number of other potential hazards to health in today's modern office which deserve some attention, although their risks are somewhat low. For example, some solvents used in typewriter correction fluids are addictive and people who regularly smell these solvents can become 'hooked'. Such 'sniffing' can be a real health hazard, causing vomiting, headaches, and so on. Thankfully, the computer age with its word processing abilities means that the use of such solvents is becoming less widespread.

Simple things such as loose carpets and trailing cables are also potential hazards which may result in serious injury. Ensure that your office is not a source of accidents by getting things like this sorted out. You can buy special cable covers which are heavy pieces of plastic to cover up trailing cables. These plastic strips will take considerable weights so people can walk on them. They are easily seen, and much more difficult to trip over than a flimsy cable. Obviously particular industries have their own intrinsic hazards and consequently have their own set of safety procedures to minimize the risks for their employees. All executives in such an industry should take great care to abide by these rules since they are set up to ensure their own safety. These safety policies are always available in writing, so make sure you and your staff have got copies of the rules and abide by them. In the UK, companies with five or more employees are required by law to provide a written policy on health matters for their staff. If you have not seen a copy, get hold of one and study it carefully. You should also have a member of staff who is qualified in first aid in case of any problems.

Food and drink

In general terms we need to be sure that we eat a balanced diet, which provides only the number of kilocalories we require each day. Many companies have canteens or executive restaurants and, sadly, research has shown that the most popular meals in these contain such items as chips, sausages, bacon, eggs, and ham. These are precisely the sort of foods which ought to be eaten very rarely as they are high in fat and cholesterol, thus increasing the chances of heart disease. In the United States, a number of companies have introduced 'healthy' menus into their staff restaurants, and research at these firms has shown that the health of the employees has improved.

Gradually companies are being encouraged to change their menus in restaurants and canteens in favour of the balanced diets recommended by doctors. One initiative has been set up by Health First, an organization offering companies a nutritional analysis of canteen meals, or the food intake of individuals, in a bid to encourage a more positive food policy amongst British companies.

Considering that some 4 million meals are eaten in company canteens each working day in the UK, and that the vast majority of them appear to be of the less healthy kind, then such encouragement is obviously a step in the right direction. Executives eating in staff restaurants, though, should adopt the advice given in earlier chapters and eat a well-balanced diet that has the right amount of kilocalories, a good proportion of protein, plenty of fibre and low levels of fat. Avoid the chips, for example, and take a baked potato instead. Have fresh fruit for your sweet, instead of ice cream. To eat a balanced diet does not mean that you need to survive on lettuce leaves and bowls of bran. You can still enjoy a varied diet, you just have to think for a second when queueing up in the canteen!

One other problem concerning food intake at work relates to the oft used and much maligned coffee machine. Next to alcohol, coffee seems to be the most widespread social drink of executives. Coffee contains caffeine, and this stimulates the production of hormones in much the same way as stress does. Consequently, caffeine ingestion can stimulate your system and fire you up ready for action. This is why many people drink coffee first thing in the morning to 'get them going'. However, too much caffeine can lead to problems, some of which are stress symptoms—irritability, nausea and digestive upsets. Headache is also a real problem for people who drink a lot of coffee. In addition even moderate levels of coffee drinking have been associated with lower levels of concentration. But how do you know if you are drinking more coffee than you should?

Caffeine is a drug; you can become 'hooked' on it. If you are addicted to caffeine you will experience a withdrawal syndrome if you have not had a cup of coffee, or tea, within the previous eighteen hours or so. This withdrawal syndrome is a craving for a coffee, as well as a severe headache. Many people experience headaches late at night, some hours after the daily caffeine fix. Others have headaches during weekends when the never ending supply of the office coffee machine is not available. This sort of addiction problem can happen with as few as four or five cups of coffee a day! Since decaffeinated coffee is available, and is also available for office vending machines, it seems a good idea to drink this instead. It will reduce the likelihood of caffeine-induced problems, such as nausea, and will also avoid any withdrawal problems like headaches.

Private medical cover

Even if an executive takes all of the precautions outlined in this book, illness may still strike. If the problem is an emergency, then it will be dealt with quickly. However if, for example, it is a chronic problem such as gallstones you may have to wait for an operation. This could mean some months of discomfort and worry. Many executives find that being backed by a private medical insurance scheme, such as that offered by BUPA or PPP, is a way of ensuring that such matters can be dealt with quickly, and with the minimal disruption to their work. Although these insurance companies cover all types of medical problem, including emergencies, for executives their value probably lies in another aspect of their work.

Companies, such as BUPA, AMI, PPP and so on, all offer 'health screening'. This is a battery of tests which can help detect early warning signs of cancer, heart disease, respiratory problems, and other health matters. The tests are performed together with a full physical examination and an interview with a doctor. The results are discussed in full and practical advice on the ways to obtain and maintain health are also provided. Executives can have these tests as often as they like—they cost around £150-£250—although every few years should be sufficient to spot most problems. Even if your company does not provide access to such schemes under a medical insurance policy, and you cannot afford, or do not wish, to take out a policy of your own these relatively inexpensive tests are well worth having done, even if they are only to stop you worrying about the problems you might, or might not, be suffering from.

In America where the medical system is almost entirely private, the regular 'check-up' is widespread. It is interesting to note that in the US there is also a falling incidence of problems such as heart disease, and many British doctors have put this down to the screening performed at the regular health check-ups.

Summary

If an executive took a wide range of steps to improve his or her health, many of these would be wasted unless the working environment was also improved. Regular exercise to avoid heart trouble would have its effects reduced if the only food available in the office canteen was laden with fats. Similarly going for a walk three times a week to reduce the chances of back trouble would be pointless if the chairs in the office were old and badly designed. Consequently all offices should be designed for the best health advantages of the staff.

This means that desks should be in appropriate positions for the doors and to gain maximum benefit from the light. Do not sit where you will cast a shadow over your work, and do not sit with your back to the door so that you have to crane your neck every time someone walks into the room. Chairs should be at the correct height so that your thighs are parallel to the floor, your weight supported on your buttocks, your knees at right angles and your feet flat on the floor. Your desk too should be at the most appropriate height for you. When working, your elbows should be by your side, your forearms parallel to the floor and your elbows at a right angle.

You should work in a well-illuminated office, which preferably should have plenty of natural light. If you use a computer, position the screen so that it is at right angles to the light source so as to avoid distracting reflections. Computers are unlikely to cause specific health hazards, since the levels of radiation they produce are remarkably small. However, they can produce an exess of positive ions in the atmosphere. These positively charged molecules have been associated with an increase in headaches, irritability and a lack of concentration. However, electric ionizers can replenish the atmosphere with the negative ions which appear to be beneficial.

Noise in the office is also a problem which can lead to irritability and may be the trigger for stress in a number of individuals. Open plan offices tend to be the noisiest, and are therefore the most difficult in which to work. Such offices may also produce minor health problems because of the small space allocated to each worker, and to the fact that desks and chairs cannot always be put in the best positions, increasing the likelihood of muscle pains because of the repeated need to move the neck and shoulders to see people and deal with the work.

Another problem with open plan offices is the possibility that smokers will pollute the entire office atmosphere, increasing the chances of non-smokers getting cancer or chronic chest diseases. The only effective answer to this problem is to ban smoking in the office. Since the majority of executives are non-smokers this may not be as unpopular as it sounds. However, a no-smoking rule needs to be adopted with care and with the full back up of medical advice which can support the smokers and help them to kick their habit.

More easily achievable is dealing with another addiction—the addiction to caffeine. This can lead to headaches and psychological problems such as anxiety. A switch from ordinary coffee to decaffeinated will help, but don't make the mistake of switching to tea; that contains caffeine too. However, caffeine-free tea is also now available.

Companies should also adopt a better policy towards the provision of healthy foods in staff canteens and executive restaurants. Many of the millions of company meals served up at the moment are not the sort which doctors would recommend as being part of a well-balanced diet. If you eat in company restaurants, and have not yet managed to convince your superiors that a change in policy is needed, then choose your meals with care. Avoid particularly fatty foods, and try to eat plenty of fruit and vegetables.

One final point about health at the workplace: take advantage of any company offer for health screening using a private medical insurance company. These 'major services' are an excellent idea, and probably deserve wider attention. If your company does not offer the scheme, then think about paying for this overhaul yourself.

| **The Healthy Workplace Plan** |

- Take a look around your office and write down any health risks you can spot, such as bad seating, poor lighting and so on.

- If possible prepare a report for seniors within the company alerting them to the problems and reminding them of their statutory obligation to protect employees' health and safety at work.

- Obtain a fully adjustable chair for your own use and set it at the correct height.

- Check that your desk is at the right height and in the best position for the light.

- Add desk lamps and standard lamps if you think they will provide helpful additional light.

- Position your VDU so that it is at right angles to light sources and so that the screen is at eye level.

- Ban smoking in your office if possible.

- Plug in an ioniser if the office is prone to regular stuffiness.

- Get acoustic hoods for printers and noise reduction pads for typewriters. If possible get the office double glazed.

- Ensure that all cables are well hidden or protected by special covers so that accidents can be avoided. Ensure that carpets fit properly.

- Keep tightly capped any solvents such as typewriter correction fluid when not in use, and monitor stock levels.

- Choose decaffeinated coffee from the drinks machine. If this is not available see if it can be obtained. If this is not possible, purchase your own supply.

- Get the canteen meals policy changed if possible. If

not, then carefully choose your meals so that a balanced diet is obtained.

- Take advantage of the regular health screening checks offered by the private medical insurance companies.

5

The Health Plan

All of the plans represented so far in this book will help an individual in his or her efforts to improve on health care in particular fields. For example, the Healthy Mind Plan is intended to help reduce stress and to create the right frame of mind for efficient working, as well as providing the motivation to tackle any of the other health plans. The Healthy Heart Plan will help lessen the risks of a heart attack, for example, as well as minimizing the risks of other disorders, including cancer. As the various parts of these health plans are interwoven, this overall plan has been prepared to draw all the strands together into a comprehensive whole. First, however, we need to understand how all of the different risk factors interact.

Stress

Even though executives do not suffer more frequently from stress than any other occupations or professions, they are still at risk of this common, complex disorder. Indeed, the effect which stress has upon our bodies should not be underestimated and trivial symptoms may be warning signs of more serious trouble ahead.

Psychological stress generally occurs as a result of feeling unsure in certain situations. We become stressed when we go for a job interview, or when we have to tell a number of people that they are being made redundant, for example. It is the uncertainty of knowing what will happen next that leads to anxiety and stress. Experience often reduces the potential for stress, but sadly, gaining this experience is stressful in itself since we have to undergo a number of different tension-inducing events to gain that experience.

As we are all different genetically, we all 'crack' under different strains. Some people can undergo a great deal more stress than others before they begin to show signs of being stressed. In the workplace the likely stresses that a particular job may create can be identified. We know, for example, that personnel managers may have to deal with a number of stress-inducing events, such as having to sack people, having to inform others about a member of staff dying, or having to discipline someone. Many personnel managers are able to cope with such stressful situations, but others, whose genetic make-up does not allow them to suffer such high levels of stress as their colleagues, may not be able to escape without symptoms, such as headaches, nausea and so on.

If only we knew the sorts of stresses that particular jobs entailed we may be able to avoid them and opt for work for which we are more temperamentally suited. Indeed, when we apply for jobs and attend interviews we are unconsciously assessing whether or not we would be able to cope. However, the career potential of some jobs can blinker us to our own weaknesses and problems which might make us less likely to be able to manage. Companies like Executive Health Screening in London offer special risk assessment questionnaires. The one produced by Executive Health Screening is a computer-based document containing 900 questions. People who wish to know if they will suit a job, or companies wishing to assess applicants, can have their answers to the hour-long survey analysed by psychologists who will say whether a person is at risk of stress in particular situations. Most of us, though, do not have the benefit of such a sophisticated method of determining whether or not we will be able to cope under the pressure of certain jobs. No doubt there are many 'misfits' in the executive world, but having established ourselves in the executive world we have to cope with it.

This means that many executives are suffering from stress because they may be genetically programmed to cope with a lower level of tension than their particular job involves. The uncertainties these executives face are likely to lead to symptoms, and if there are any conflicts between people, problems at home, or difficulties in apportioning time, then the stress will increase and the symptoms become more serious.

As was explained in Chapter 1, there is sound biological evidence to support the theory that stress does lead to symptoms. The response to a stressful situation is an automatic increase in a complex array of hormones which prepare our bodies to deal head-on with the stressful factor, or to be able to run away quickly from it. If we were to do either of those things—we might run away from an escaped tiger, for example—then the body would stop the hormone production quickly and bring us back to normal as soon as the threat ceased. Sadly, psychological stressors do not always allow us to attack them immediately, or to run away from them. Consequently our bodies can end up in an unnatural state of constant readiness for 'fight or flight', unable to 'switch-off' and leaving us prone to the symptoms of stress. The hormones released during our response to stress have a number of different effects: they take away blood from our digestive system, halting digestion; they sharpen our senses; they refine our concentration so that we can only think of the problem in hand; they prime our muscles ready for action; and they increase our heart and breathing rates. It is therefore only a short step from these changes in our body's natural state to one of stress symptoms.

The sorts of symptoms produced have been explained in detail in 'A Healthy Mind', and include irritability, chest pains, lack of sex drive, insomnia and so on. However, taking into account all of the other facets of health discussed so far in this book, it is possible to see how stress plays a central role in the overall health of executives.

A stressful situation creates a number of effects: one of these is to heighten our senses. Consequently any executive under stress is more likely to be aware of office noise, such as loud computer printers, the hum of fluorescent light fittings, the constant ringing of tele-phones and so on. As we saw in Chapter 4 'A Healthy Workplace' these are precisely the sorts of environmental problems which *cause* stress. So a stressed person is likely to become even more stressed if the office environment is not right. A stressed person may also become more stressed by noise at home, such as a newborn baby crying during the night.

Another factor in stress seems to be diet, as discussed in Chapters 1 and 4. In this latter chapter it was shown that caffeine can induce symptoms of stress. So an executive who is addicted to coffee—as few as four or five cups a day—and who is under stress is likely to be increasing the severity of any symptoms, or making them more likely to develop. The avoidance of stress therefore requires conversion to decaffeinated coffee.

As was shown in Chapter 2 'A Healthy Heart', stress is also an important risk factor for heart disease. The hormonal changes induced by continual stress increase the amount of fats which contain cholesterol in the blood, causing the arteries to become clogged. It is this problem which is known to be the main cause of heart and circulatory disorders. However, as was shown in Chapter 1, illness itself is something which causes us stress. Consequently anyone who has heart disease may well make the problem worse! The knowledge of the illness induces stress which adds to the risk of heart disease! Avoiding this vicious circle can only really effectively be achieved by preventing heart disease in the first place.

Heart disease

As we have seen, heart disease can be caused by stress. However, as was explained in Chapter 2, it is more likely to be caused by smoking. Since the World Health

Organization has declared passive smoking a positive risk to health, even non-smokers may be at risk of heart disease if they are inhaling smoke regularly in the environment. This links 'A Healthy Heart' with 'A Healthy Workplace'. Open plan offices which allow executives to smoke could be putting the health of all workers at risk, and no matter how many steps individuals might take in caring for their health, their attempts could be negated by the smoke they inhaled at work.

Diet is also linked to heart disease, and so office canteens and executive restaurants really ought to provide healthy menus which contain less fats than many of the traditional canteen meals, often accompanied by chips!

A lack of exercise is thought to be behind an increased risk of heart disease too. Exercise has been shown to reduce the levels of harmful fats in the bloodstream, so reducing the chances of a build up of cholesterol and a clogging up of the arteries. However, Chapter 3, 'A Healthy Body' explained that exercise is also of value in preventing muscular and skeletal problems, such as backache—the most common cause of days off work in the UK. Consequently, someone who looks after their heart by exercising will also be helping to protect their back.

However, that effort will be wasted if proper chairs and desks are not provided within the office, which only goes to emphasize the importance of the environment within which we live and work. Executives will find, therefore, that other factors in their working environment may affect their disease status.

Take, for example, hotels. Executives regularly use hotels; indeed in researching this book it was discovered that more than 50 per cent of hotel guests are staying on business. An increasing number of hotels have begun to provide healthy menus in their restaurants, and health and fitness facilities are provided so that exercise programmes may be continued whilst away from home, thus both reducing the chances of heart disease. Many of the more aware hotel chains (these have been mentioned in Chapter 2), have also introduced no-smoking bedrooms and public areas in which smoking is banned. However, as any conference visitor will know, many hotels do not provide the most comfortable of chairs for meetings. So even though hotel management is taking major steps forward in the direction of reducing our chances of heart and circulatory disease, their control of our environment is not always helping our backs. Nevertheless, in recent years attitudes have changed and the steps taken by hotels should not be underestimated; they are very important in helping us achieve an improved health status. However, there are other areas which will help disease and conditions which are not related to our hearts.

Cancer

Cancer is the third largest killer of executives. Heart disease is the most common, then comes other circulatory problems such as strokes, then cancer. Cancer kills one person in every five. Unlike many instances of heart disease induced death, the dying of a cancer sufferer is rarely sudden. It is a slow and painful process. This is behind the fear we all have of cancer, but the prevention of a large chunk of the statistics is possible by taking similar steps to preventing heart disease.

Firstly, do not smoke, and avoid all smoky atmospheres. Lung cancer kills more people than any other kind, and now more women suffer from this type of cancer, even more than from the much-feared breast cancer. It is not insignificant that the incidence of female lung cancer has risen along with an increase in the number of women smoking. So by cutting out smoking we will not only be reducing our chances of heart disease, as explained in 'A Healthy Heart', but also of cutting down the risk of cancer as outlined in 'A Healthy Body'. Similarly, alterations in our diet will be likely to reduce our risk of contracting cancer, in addition to helping our heart. And the central problem of stress also returns in cancer, since animal experiments have shown that stress is linked to an increased incidence of cancer. So taking steps to reduce stress will not only cut down the heart disease risk which besets so many executives, but may also limit their chances of contracting cancer.

Gastrointestinal problems

Stress is also linked to disturbances of the digestive system, as outlined in both 'A Healthy Mind' and 'A Healthy Body'. The removal of blood from the digestive tract during our response to stressors means that digestion effectively stops. When the stress is over, it starts up again. With constant stress this stop-start effect on the digestion can be at the root of difficulties. Indigestion can occur, stomach ulcers may begin to form, and the irritable bowel syndrome may take a hold. Sadly, many executives who have these troubles make them worse. The stress which may cause such problems in the first place is frequently relieved by smoking and/or drinking alcohol. However, these two addictions are also known to affect the digestive system.

Smoking, for example is strongly linked to the formation of ulcers since it reduces the protective chemicals, called prostaglandins, which are produced in the stomach. Smoking therefore not only affects our chances of heart disease and cancer, but also of gastrointestinal disorders. Smoking as a result of stress provides an example of how factors outlined in 'A Healthy Mind' are interconnected with material in 'A Healthy Body'. Only by reducing stress will people who smoke to relieve tension be able to kick their habit and so cut down their chances of suffering from these various diseases.

Diet too has an influence on our intestines. A lack of fibre, for example, has been linked to the development of cancer of the bowel. Fibre helps in the transport of foodstuffs and residue through our digestive tract; it allows for a much smoother and rather faster journey. A properly balanced diet will contain sufficient fibre for these needs—there is no need to eat barrels of bran every day. Such a balanced diet, though, is of importance in the prevention of heart disease, as explained in 'A Healthy Heart'. A good diet is also of major importance in the prevention of obesity. Being overweight is not only likely to cause heart disease, it is also a common precursor of diabetes. Also, people who are overweight die younger than their normal weight colleagues.

Summary

It is possible to see that there is a wide variety of conditions, diseases and health problems which can be caused by the interaction of a large number of different factors. Simply giving attention to one of the risk factors, whilst being of some value, will not be truly helpful unless all of the other matters which increase risk are also dealt with.

It is also possible to see that each risk factor to our health, also influences more than one of our bodily systems and may therefore give rise to more than one kind of illness. Since we do not know our own individual, genetically pre-determined likelihood to suffer from particular diseases then in order to improve our health status we really need to assume that we are at risk of all problems. We therefore need first of all to put ourselves in the right frame of mind to do something positive about our health.

The first step to health improvement is in changing our attitude of mind. We can only really do this, however, when we have a clear perspective of the problems we have and the likely problems from which we could suffer. The first step in an overall health improvement must be a self-audit. We must take stock and assess our own situation in detail. The Health Questionnaire in the next chapter will help in this process. You will need to sit down one evening and complete this questionnaire carefully, thinking all the time of any special circumstances which may apply to you. It may be helpful to get a spouse, relative or friend to help you answer the questions more objectively—we are notoriously dishonest with ourselves!

Having completed the self-assessment with the help of the questionnaire, you should then be able to see more clearly the health risks that you are taking. You will therefore know whether or not you are likely to be prone to stress, for example, or heart disease. Whatever your particular risks are you should follow the plan most appropriate to that area—if you are a stress sufferer, for example, follow 'The Healthy Mind Plan'. Re-read the chapter which is most relevant to your needs.

Having reached this far, make an appointment to see your doctor. Whilst there may be nothing wrong with you and you may feel in perfect health, you should always inform your doctor of any attempts to change your lifestyle. There may be some steps you take which could be dangerous if you have a pre-existing medical condition. For example, people who already have some degree of heart disease should not start an exercise programme unless their family doctor has said it would be reasonable to do so. Sudden exercise in such people may bring on a heart attack.

Seeing your doctor is also a good idea since general practitioners will be able to check your general health and provide you with any other advice specific to you. Family doctors will also be able to monitor your progress as you follow any positive health plan, making sure that you are obtaining and maintaining an improved health status. You should not underestimate the value of a general practitioner, and you really should seek their advice before adopting any of the health plans in this book—not that they are dangerous, but they are provided for the average general population, and you might not be so 'average'!

Once you have seen your doctor you will be ready to follow the particular health-promoting plans most appropriate to your needs. However, for most executives all of the plans should be followed. This is why this final chapter includes an overall Health Plan. Having assessed what you need to change in your lifestyle and sought approval from your doctor, you should then 'announce' that you intend to become a more healthy individual. Let your family, friends and work colleagues know what you are doing. If you do not, they will wonder why on earth you have suddenly taken to walking everywhere, or using the stairs instead of the lift. Friends will be able to prepare you low fat meals for dinner parties, without being embarrassed by you leaving something on the plate! Your spouse will not think that you have started an affair because of your twice weekly visit to the swimming pool. And your children will not think you've blown a gasket when you take your 20 minutes relaxation every day after work. By informing all of your friends and relatives in this way, it will help you adopt the plans. Their encouragement and comments will also help you stick to the plans!

Telling colleagues at work will also help, since you will no doubt be soliciting support for smoking restrictions, improvements in the canteen menu, and better chairs. You may have to do a bit of campaigning on this, but if you are a senior executive with the necessary power, then there is no reason why you cannot improve the health status of your colleagues by putting a few of the 'Healthy Workplace' suggestions into practice.

Once all that is done you will be ready to begin to follow any of the special health plans to improve your lifestyle. However, just one assessment and a few simple changes will not be enough. You will need to monitor your progress regularly—once a month should be sufficient in the early stages. You also ought to contact your doctor again, either to pass on information about your progress, or to ask for help and advice with any particular areas. Smokers, for example, will require assistance to give up.

After a few months your new way of life will become so natural, and almost certainly more enjoyable, that you will hardly be able to remember those unhealthy days before. All you need to do is follow the simple Executive Health Plan. Good Luck!

The Executive Health Plan

- Arrange a time when you and a relative or friend can sit down and take stock of your current lifestyle and health situation. Complete the Health Questionnaire in the next chapter.

- Assess your current health status and analyse which areas will need attention if you are at risk of certain conditions and illnesses.

- Re-read the relevant chapters of this book to focus your mind on the issues.

- Tell your family, friends and colleagues that you are determined to make alterations in your lifestyle to improve your health.

- Set some rules which will help you to do this, such as not being disturbed during relaxation sessions.

- See your doctor before you take any further action. Tell your family practitioner what you plan to do and seek further specific advice and encouragement.

- Seek support from colleagues and superiors for improving the workplace.

- Start an effective method of time management. Either buy a pre-packed system or devise your own. All that really matters is you write down your goals at work and in your personal life, and give deadlines for the achievement of those targets. The system should also include all of your daily, weekly, monthly and annual appointments. In addition it should allow you to allot space for other matters such as reading, writing and so on. The system should be able to provide you with a flexible timetable.

- Discuss your sex life with your partner, and think about improving it and/or, making it more exciting; go away for a long weekend on a 'sexual holiday', for example.

- Perform a daily ritual of relaxation after coming home from work.

- Start a diet and lose weight if you are obese. Check your ideal weight by looking at Table 5 (pages 59 and 60).

- Adopt a sensible approach to eating. Eat a low fat, high fibre diet. Avoid sugary foods, and if you have high blood pressure avoid salt. Try, whenever possible, to eat three meals a day. This will stop you 'picking' and devouring snacks.

- Control your drinking habits. Count your drinks over a period of a fortnight and keep a diary of your drinking activities. If you had more than 12 pints of beer, or equivalent, you need to cut down.

- Give up smoking, immediately and permanently. Avoid all smoky atmospheres. Do not allow smoking in your office or in your home. Seek medical help to ensure that you quit. If necessary consider chewing gum nicotine prescribed by doctors as a temporary replacement for the habit.

- Assess your behaviour patterns, and if you are a Type A individual seek ways of changing your behaviour (see Table 4, pages 54 and 55). Get specialist help if necessary.

- Perform at least 1 hour of exercise each week. This is best done in three 20-minute sessions. Do some warm up stretching and bending before each exercise session. Walking is an ideal exercise, so too is swimming.

- Perform monthly self-examination procedures to check for cancer.

- Be aware of the threat of AIDS. Outside a regular and wholly monogamous relationship, ALWAYS use a condom during sexual activity.

- Obtain information from hotels about diets, no-smoking areas, and exercise facilities. Make a note in your time management system of the hotels most appropriate for your needs which offer these extra

facilities. Don't book anywhere else if you can
possibly avoid it.

- Assess the menus of restaurants to which you take
  business clients. Only go to those which offer good,
  balanced and healthy meals.

- Attend to the furniture in your office and if
  necessary improve chairs, desks, lighting, heating,
  ventilation and noise. If necessary add an ioniser or
  an air purifier.

- Follow any specific safety precautions applying to
  the industry in which you work.

- Obtain a regular health screen from a reputable
  agency, such as BUPA, PPP or AMI.

In short:

- Assess your current lifestyle and prepare to make
  changes.

- Adopt an efficient time management system.

- Stop smoking.

- Control your alcohol intake.

- Lose weight if necessary.

- Adopt a sensible balanced diet.

- Take regular exercise.

- Relax each day.

6

Health Questionnaire

The following questions should be used as the basis for a self-audit when trying to assess your own health status. This questionnaire is not exhaustive and there may be particular areas in your life not covered by these questions. However, they should give you a general guide as to the likely risks you are taking and will help you see more clearly the areas in your life which need changing if you are to improve successfully your health status.

1   Do you smoke?

2   How many years have you smoked?

3   If you do not smoke do you frequently visit smoky atmospheres?

4   Do you drink alcohol on more than three occasions each week?

5   Do you regularly drink alcohol alone?

6   Do you always need an alcoholic drink to overcome the tensions of the day?

7   Are you ambitious?

8   Are you ever accused of shouting, or speaking too quickly?

9   Do you drive at speed?

10   Are you keen to get things done, and then move on to the next task as soon as possible?

11   Do you eat breakfast?

12   Is the breakfast you eat a 'traditional English' breakfast of bacon, eggs, sausages, etc?

13   Do you need to start the day with a cup of coffee to 'get you going'?

14   Do you drink more than four cups of coffee each day?

15   Do you regularly skip a lunch break?

16   Do you frequently miss a lunchtime meal?

17   Is a normal lunchtime spent in a public house?

18   During 'business luncheons' do you always eat three courses?

19   Do you carefully consider menus in restaurants and hotels?

20   Do you relax at the end of each day?

21   Do you become tense and irritable?

22   Do you get angry in business meetings?

23   Do you do any kind of regular exercise?

24   Do you 'warm-up' before exercise?

25   Are you within the accepted weight range for your height? (See Table 5, pages 59 and 60.)

26   Do you eat red meat, eggs, butter, chips and sweet foods on a regular basis?

27   Do you add salt to every meal, even though you know you may be suffering from high blood pressure?

28   Do you find that you never have enough time to do all of the things you would like to do?

29   Do you find noise in the office unacceptable at times?

30 Are your desk and chair appropriate for your height?

31 Do you sit up straight in chairs, or do you lounge about?

32 Do you have an enjoyable sex life?

33 Do you always use condoms when engaging in sexual activity outside a truly monogamous relationship?

34 Do you ensure that you are properly vaccinated for trips abroad?

35 Do you suffer from any of the following symptoms: Regular cough; irregular bowel habit; indigestion; breathlessness?

36 Do you regularly examine yourself, or get checked by a doctor, for possible signs of cancer?

37 Do you have close relatives who have suffered from heart disease?

38 Do you have close relatives who have suffered from cancer?

39 Did your parents die young as a result of illness?

40 Are you constantly worried about your health?

Assessing your replies

If you replied 'Yes' to Question 1 you are seriously risking your overall health. You are likely to die younger than you should and you may get heart disease or cancer. The risks are greater if you have smoked for a number of years. Your answer to Question 2 will help you put into perspective the risks you are taking. Question 3 has been included because there is evidence that even non-smokers can be harmed by the effects of a smoky atmosphere.

If you answered 'Yes' to Questions 4, 5 and 6, then you

are likely to be damaging your liver. You may also be harming your heart since positive replies to these questions suggest you are under some degree of stress.

Positive responses to Questions 7 to 10 show that you exhibit Type A behaviour patterns and are therefore more likely to suffer from heart disease.

If you answered 'No' to Question 11 it shows that you may be stressed because you rush out of the house without allowing time for breakfast. It also implies that you may easily become overweight, with all the attendant risks, because you will make up for the skipped meal later during the day.

If you replied 'Yes' to Question 12 you are eating a poorly balanced menu. Your fat intake is probably too high. This will increase your chances of heart disease.

If you said 'Yes to Questions 13 and 14 you may be addicted to caffeine. This could be the cause of some non-specific complaints such as headaches.

Questions 15 to 17 will show that you are at an increased risk of heart and liver disease if you replied 'Yes'. Skipping lunches may mean that you are under too much pressure and unable to take time out of the office. This extra degree of stress may lead to various complaints, and may be linked to heart disease. If you regularly spend your lunchbreak in a public house you may well be consuming a dangerously high level of alcohol.

If you answered 'Yes' to Question 18, you are probably overeating leading to obesity. You may well also be having too high a fat intake, thus further increasing the chances of heart disease. If you said 'Yes' to Question 19 then you are behaving in a healthy manner, providing you choose meals which are balanced.

Question 20 will show that you are at increased risk of stress-related illnesses if you answered 'No'. If you answered 'Yes' to Questions 21 and 22 this confirms that you are probably suffering from some degree of stress.

If you answered 'No' to Questions 23 and 24 you are going to be at an increased risk of heart disease, and musculo-skeletal complaints. Warming up prior to exercise is necessary to help you realize the maximum benefit of exercise, and will also be of some use in helping to prevent muscle strains.

If your answer to Question 25 was 'No' then you should lose weight. An obese person dies earlier than someone in their ideal weight range and also stands a greater chance of having heart disease or diabetes. They may also be more prone to back trouble.

A positive reply to Questions 26 and 27 shows that you are probably not eating a balanced diet. You are increasing your chances of heart disease, and possibly of cancer.

If you answered 'Yes' to Questions 28 and 29 your stress levels may be too high.

Saying 'Yes' to Questions 30 and 31 shows that you may be damaging your back and neck.

If you said 'No' to Question 32 you may well be suffering from tension and stress. Your relationship may also be in difficulty which will add to any of the other problems you are experiencing and making you less able to cope.

An answer of 'No' to Question 33 is downright dangerous and irresponsible. It is the only practical way we have of curbing the spread of AIDS. To avoid this simple precaution means that you are seriously damaging your health, and the health of your sexual partners.

You may also be generally risking your health if you answered 'No' to Question 34.

If you suffered from any of the symptoms listed in Question 35 you may already be suffering from troubles in the lungs, the digestive system and the heart. Some of these symptoms may also indicate that you are suffering from stress. If you suffer from any of these you should seek medical attention.

If you answered 'Yes' to Question 36 you will be increasing the likelihood of successful treatment should a cancer be found. If you answered 'No' you may well miss the development of cancer.

If you answered 'Yes' to Questions 37 to 39 you may be at an increased risk of certain disorders. A number of conditions tend to 'run in families'. If you have relatives who have suffered from these problems, you may well be more likely to develop the conditions. You should therefore take special care of yourself to further reduce the likelihood.

Finally, if you said 'No' to Question 40, congratulations. There is no need to be constantly worried about your health. If you replied 'Yes' you should seek medical advice so that you can be comforted that there is no serious trouble. There have also been some suggestions that those people who worry that they will suffer from cancer tend to have cancers more commonly than people who do not worry.

Summary

This questionnaire is not intended to be the most comprehensive guide to your own health status. It is merely provided to stimulate you into thinking about your own health. This is why no 'points system' has been allocated to the questionnaire, as the intention is not to grade your health status in some arbitrary and generalized scale of risks. This questionnaire, though, will show you general areas of your life which may need some attention if you want to improve your health status, and direct you to those health plans presented in the book which might be of most use to you.

Further Reading

Diet and Cardiovascular Disease, Committee on Medical Aspects of Food Policy, Report of the Panel on Diet in Relation to Cardiovascular Disease, HMSO, London, 1984.

The New E for Additives, by Maurice Hanssen, Thorsons Publishing Group, Wellingborough, 1987.

Ease and Disease: How to Achieve Permanent Good Health, by Dr Beric Wright, Longman, London, 1986.

Everybody: A Nutritional Guide to Life, by Derek Llewellyn Jones, Oxford University Press, Oxford, 1980.

Executive Stress, by Donald Norfolk, Arrow Books, London, 1986.

Exercise: The Facts, by E. J. Bassey and P. H. Fentem, Oxford University Press, Oxford, 1981

How to Survive the 9-5, by Martin Lucas, Kim Wilson and Emma Hart, Thames Methuen, London, 1986.

Nature and Treatment of the Stress Response, The, by George Everly Jr and Robert Rosenfeld, The Plenum Press, New York, 1981.

Nutrition, Diet and Health, by Michael J. Gibney, Cambridge University Press, Cambridge, 1986.

Office Work Can Be Dangerous To Your Health, by Jeanne Stellman and Mary Sue Henifin, Pantheon Books, New York, 1983.

Pre-Menstrual Syndrome, The, by Dr Caroline Shreeve, Thorsons Publishing Group, Wellingborough, 1983.

Prevention and Health: Everybody's Business, Department of Health and Social Security, HMSO, London, 1981.

Smoking and Health, Royal College of Physicians, Pitman Publishing, London 1962.

Smoking and Health, Public Health Service Publication No. 1103, US Department of Health and Human Sciences, 1964.

Smoking and Health, Public Health Service Publication No. 79-50066, US Department of Health, Education and Welfare, 1979.

Stress and the Woman Manager, by Marylin Davidson and Cary Cooper, Martin Robertson & Co., Oxford, 1983.

Stress in Industry, by Joseph Kearns, Priory Press, London, 1973.

Time for Success, by James Noon, International Thomson Publishing Ltd, London, 1983.

Traveller's Health Guide, The, by Dr Anthony Turner, Roger Lascelles, Brentford, 1985.

Understanding Executive Stress, by Cary Cooper and Judi Marshall, Macmillan Press, London, 1978.

Work and Health, by Andrew Melhuish, Penguin Handbooks, Harmondsworth, 1982.

Working Well, by Marjorie Blanchard and Mark Tager, Wildwood House, Aldershot, 1986.

Working Woman: A Guide to Fitness and Health, by Anita Shreve and Patricia Lone, the C. V. Mosby Company, St Louis, USA, 1986.

Writing Your Health and Safety Policy, Health and Safety Commission, HMSO, London 1986.

Useful Addresses

The following list of organizations may be helpful to executives who wish to learn more about specific aspects of health.

Alcohol Concern
305 Gray's Inn Road, London, WC1X 8QF.
Charity which promotes controlled drinking habits and has initiated a Workplace Project to help companies and individuals get to grips with work-related drinking.

Alcoholics Anonymous
PO Box 514, 11 Radcliffe Gardens, London, SW10 9BQ.
Offers help and advice for people with a drink problem. Local telephone numbers for confidential help are given in the telephone directory.

AMI Health Care
4 Cornwall Terrace, London, NW1 4QP.
Runs private hospitals and offers executive health screening service.

Back Pain Association
31-33 Park Road, Teddington, Middx, TW11 0AB.
Promotes back pain research and provides constructive help on dealing with back problems.

British Diabetic Association
10 Queen Anne Street, London, W1M 0BD.
Offers help and advice for diabetics.

British Heart Foundation
102 Gloucester Place, London, W1H 4DH.
Promotes research into heart disease. Has produced a 'cost calculator' which works out the financial losses caused to companies as a result of heart disease.

British Migraine Association
178a High Road, Byfleet, Weybridge, Surrey, KT14 7ED.
Promotes research and gives advice and help to sufferers.

British Rheumatism and Arthritis Association
6 Grosvenor Crescent, London, SW1X 7ER.

BUPA
Provident House, Essex Street, London, WC2R 3AX.
Health insurance, hospitals and health screening.

CancerLink
46 Pentonville Road, London, N1 9HF.
Provides information and advice for cancer sufferers and their families.

The Chest Heart and Stroke Association
Tavistock House North, Tavistock Square, London, WC1H 9JE.
Promotes research into chest and cardiovascular disease, as well as providing information to sufferers.

Executive Health Screening
45 Nottingham Place, London, W1.
Offers stress-assessment computerised questionnaire, as well as full medical and counselling facilities for companies and individuals.

Family Planning Association
27-35 Mortimer Street, London, W1N 7RJ.
Provides advice on contraception and family planning.

Health and Safety Executive
St Hughes House, Stanley Precinct, Bootle, L20 3QY.
Oversees the operation of the Health and Safety at Work
Acts.

Health First
Richmond Hill, Bournemouth, BH2 6EQ.
Offers a variety of company health services, including a
special analysis of menus provided by canteens.

Mind
The National Association for Mental Health, 22 Harley
Street, London, W1N 2ED.

National Society for Cancer Relief
30 Dorset Square, London, NW1 6QL.

Organization for Parents Under Stress (OPUS)
106 Godstone Road, Whyteleafe, Croydon, CR3 0EB.

The Pre-Retirement Association
19 Undine Street, London, SW17 8PP.

Private Patients Plan (PPP)
Tavistock House South, Tavistock Square, London,
WC1H 9LJ.
Private medical insurance and health screening.

Stress Syndrome Foundation
Cedar House, Yalding, Kent, ME18 6JD.
Offers course for companies on stress management.

Terrence Higgins Trust
BM AIDS, London, WC1N 3XX.
Offers counselling and advice on AIDS.

Women's National Cancer Control Campaign
1 South Audley Street, London, W1Y 5DQ.

The Yoga for Health Foundation
Ickwell Bury, Nr Biggleswade, Bedfordshire.
Can provide information on local groups.

UNITED STATES

Alliance for the Mentally Ill
1997 Highway PB, Verona, Wisconsin, 53593.

American Cancer Society
777 Third Avenue, New York, NY 10017.

American Diabetes Association
600 Fifth Avenue, New York, NY 10020.

American Heart Association
7320 Greenville Ave, Dallas, TX 75231.

American Rheumatism Association
3400 Peachtree Road NE, Atlanta, GA 30326.

National Association for Mental Health
1800 N Kent Street, Arlington, VA 22209.

National Council on Alcoholism
733 Third Ave, New York, NY 10017.

National High Blood Pressure Education Program
1501 Wilson Blvd, Arlington, VA 22298.

AUSTRALIA

Association of Relatives and Friends of the Mentally Ill
165 Blues Point Road, Momahon's Point, New South
Wales 2060.

Australian Cancer Society
PO Box 4708, Sydney, New South Wales 2001.

Australian Foundation for Alcoholism and Drug Dependence
PO Box 477, Canberra 2601.

Australian Rheumatism Association
145 Macquarie Street, Sydney, New South Wales 2000.

National Heart Foundation of Australia
PO Box 2, Woden, Australian Capital Territory 2606.

Index

Of further interest . . .

Be the Most Effective Manager in Your Business

Do you devote most of your time and experience to your own particular area of expertise at the expense of using your managerial skills? Using that managerial ability will enable you to employ your expertise profitably.

Learn to: manage yourself; communicate with other people; manage your own staff.

If you are in a managerial or executive position in any business organization and want to become more effective, then this book is for you.

John Lockett has many years' experience in personnel. He has worked with, trained and developed managers at all levels in the chemical, food and retail industries.